WIN
YOUR
BREAKUP

WIN YOUR BREAKUP

HOW TO BE THE ONE THAT GOT AWAY

NATASHA ADAMO

LIONCREST
PUBLISHING

COPYRIGHT © 2021 BY NATASHA ADAMO

All rights reserved. Unauthorized duplication is a violation of applicable law. For more information, go to the author's website at www.natashaadamo.com.

WIN YOUR BREAKUP
How to Be The One That Got Away

ISBN 978-1-5445-2279-1 *Hardcover*
      978-1-5445-2278-4 *Paperback*
      978-1-5445-2774-1 *Ebook*
      978-1-5445-2280-7 *Audiobook*

"A masterclass in self-respect and dropping the mic on a toxic ex."

—Greg Behrendt, #1 *New York Times* bestselling co-author of *He's Just Not That Into You*

To my younger self.
Everything I am and do is for you.

To my best friend, my Mom.
The original White Horse warrior.

And to YOU.
I know exactly how defeated, discarded,
and alone you feel right now.
The doormat era of your life ENDS the
moment you turn this page.

CONTENTS

Part 1
THE MINDSET OF A WINNER

Part 2
THE WISDOM OF A WINNER

Part 3
WINNING YOUR BREAKUP

WHO THIS BOOK IS FOR

This book is for YOU. It is written as though I am speaking directly to you because I am. I see myself in you; I see my own experiences and pain in yours. There is not a word I have written in this book where you were not on my mind.

How am I so sure that this book is for you?

You would never have picked up a book called *Win Your Breakup* if your breakup had not been **reduced** to what feels like a game that you now have to "win" to emotionally survive and move on. And that reduction can only take place if you are going through a breakup with a *toxic* person. Anyone who gets validation by exploiting your hunger for theirs is, in my opinion, **toxic**—to *your* peace, *your* life, and *your* mental health.

Winning your breakup is not about acting on vengeful feelings, becoming a carrot-dangling tactician, or playing games. It's about a willingness to do what you have never done before and having the courage to look in the mirror. It's about using spiteful feelings to your *dignified* advantage after realizing you've invested in a dead end.

Unlike a game, breakups are won through resignation. They're won by giving up on trying to make sense out of nonsense. They're won by realizing that the real "win" was *losing* a partner who does not have the ability to meet you anywhere close to halfway. This mentality is what dismantles toxic people. They don't know what to do when everything they relied on to feel powerful and significant is no longer there. Starting with your low self-esteem, lack of boundaries, and desperation for a crumb of their attention.

A new identity and existence are waiting for you at the end of this journey. A life with relationships that you don't have to tolerate, apologize, and eggshell walk your way through. A life where you can call your own relational shots. A life where your ex regrets the day they *ever* decided to breach your trust and break your heart. A life where those who took you for granted wish you could find a way back into theirs. A life where you can choose to walk *away* from toxicity—instead of trying to be whatever someone *may* want, *may* commit to, *may* be honest with, and *may* treat with respect.

That life is about to be your own.

And although I can lead you to everything that you know you want and deserve, the one thing I cannot do is control how hungry you are for better—a better relationship with yourself, first and foremost, and a better life. The problem is, better is not familiar, and the unfamiliar is scary. But I am here with you, each and every step of the way.

You will learn more about me throughout this journey, but I want to make it very clear that my education has not come from a classroom, a certification program, or a license of any kind. It has come from my own life experiences. I do not speak from any kind of psychological high horse, nor do I claim to know all the answers.

But I have been in your shoes. I have gone through breakups that have left me suicidal and made me feel like I had no choice but to abandon my dignity, moral code, and intuition—just so I could get more time with an ex who had no problem wasting mine. I know what it's like to feel completely defeated, emotionally knocked down, and left for dead.

I also know what it's like to experience the kind of freedom and satisfaction of getting up off the ground in a way no one *ever* thought I could.

Now it's your turn.

THE DEAL

This book is written from the perspective of a straight woman (me). I cannot authentically write from any perspective or experience other than my own. However, I am honored to have coached thousands of people around the world and to have many readers from the LGBTQ Community. Everyone struggles with the same confusion, pain, and toxicity—it's just different body parts and dynamics. The common denominators are always the same, and our pain is what connects us all.

Choosing to give that pain a *purpose* is what makes us family.

Although I write from the perspective of a straight woman, what I write about does not discriminate against gender, orientation, age, or stage in life. I do not, in any way, want to exclude *anyone* from this conversation.

Additionally, I have a huge problem with and no respect for people who engage in male-bashing. Men are NOT the problem. Toxicity is the problem, self-hatred is the problem, un-dealt with trauma is the problem—not men.

Going through a breakup with a toxic person is pretty awful no matter what gender they are or what type of relationship it is. Of course, I want *everyone*—not just women—to win their breakup. I want everyone to benefit from what I have learned and put into this book with all the love in my heart. But because I have only been in romantic relationships with men, I use "he" throughout this book. Please know where my heart lies here. Forgive me for not including the specific pronoun that applies to your relationship and always adjust accordingly.

This material is not solely intended for people going through a breakup with a toxic ex in a romantic relationship. It can be applied to a breakup with a toxic friend, a coworker, even a family member.

I am not a way-shower of any kind, nor am I a licensed or certified professional in anything. As I said in the last section, my knowledge comes from experience, not a formal education.

What you are about to read is a powerful guide, but only *you* know the way. **Me pretending to know what's best for you would dim the one thing that I have dedicated my life to amplifying:** you listening to and acting on *your* intuition, not being dependent on me and mine.

Give yourself a chance to absorb this material. I have found that sadly, it is much easier to be relationally conned and manipulated than it is to get someone to act on the acceptance that they've been conned and manipulated. We are conditioned to make other people's behavior (or lack thereof) about us and our value when it never was and never will be the case.

Throughout this book, I occasionally use curse words because, throughout the day, when I speak, I occasionally use those same words. These specific words become unprofessional and problematic when used to cover for an inability to express oneself, provide "shock value," and offend others. I think that these words can be classified as "bad" when they are used in an effort to perpetuate hate, ignorance, and division. I, nongratuitously, use them with absolutely no disrespect to anyone but as a form of emphasis. And also because this is how I authentically speak. I never want to do both you and me the disservice of changing or editing my voice just because it's written in a book.

There are no case studies in this book, no examples with made-up people or real-life clients. If you were having a heart attack right now and got rushed to the hospital, would you want the doctor to come in and present case studies and examples to you? Or would you want immediate help?

I am not a doctor, but this book, this *playbook*, is immediate emotional defibrillation—with all the attention on YOU—100 percent of the time. It is delivered with compassion and immediacy because I know that this is, quite literally, a matter of emotional life and death.

Part 1

THE
MINDSET
OF A
WINNER

Without Death, There Are No Ashes to Rise From

How to Remember Who the Fuck You Are

The first thing you need to do after a breakup is remember who the fuck you are. But how can you remember what you need to when you were in a relationship that required you to forget what you could not afford to forget (your strength, your standards, and yourself)?

How could this happen after you gave so much and asked for so little?

Why wasn't it enough? Why weren't *you* enough?

There's nothing wrong with thinking about everything you did for your ex. Hindsight only becomes blinding when it's not grounded in reality. The reality is, *you* hold the value here—not someone whose sense of worth comes from getting you to question your own.

Think of the *value* in everything that you gave, excused, believed in, and took the time to explain.

Do you know how much of a rarity that is?

In a dating world of instant gratification, immature games, entitlement, and a lack of old-school values, *you gave*—with all of your heart.

You had a winning lottery ticket in a sea of ticket holders. And when it came time to grow those riches mutually, your ex choked. He wasn't ready to handle the level of wealth you were so willing to share. Not because your riches weren't "good enough" to ignite an appreciation for all that you are and gave, but because, after a while, those riches began to highlight his bankruptcy. He could no longer keep up the charade.

And when someone's insecurities run that deep, walking away will always be easier than having to look in the mirror.

For him to win this breakup, your ex needs three things (three things that *all* toxic people need to survive):

- Your attention

- Your reaction

- Your low self-esteem

For you to win this breakup, you need to do three things (three things that he is convinced you are incapable of doing):

- Maintain silence.

- Activate indifference.

- Remember who the fuck you are.

But right now, you are stuck in the most painful and confusing limbo.

> **You are caught between the hope of resuscitating the man you miss (the man he was in the beginning) and the acceptance of that man no longer having a pulse.**

Death is something that we are not wired to ever get used to. We are, however, wired to accept and heal in the finality associated with it. When a loved one physically dies, it is the most unnatural and excruciating feeling in this world. But at least we can mourn without having to wonder if and when they will physically return.

You are now experiencing the one thing that can feel even harder to get over than the loss associated with physical death: mourning the death of someone you thought you knew—*as they live and breathe in a life that seems so much better without you in it.*

Letting go of someone you love is hard enough. Having to accept their death while knowing that they are still walking the earth is soul shattering—no matter how much better you know you deserve.

Any attempts you make to resuscitate your relationship with a toxic ex will backfire. The resulting embarrassment will drain you of your self-respect and strengthen your self-sabotaging beliefs. This experience turns you into a magnet for more relationships that are just as unfulfilling as the one you have with yourself.

Your triggers will try everything to justify acting on desperation by getting you to believe in a pulse that does not exist—all while everyone looks on at the unfortunate dummy who's trying to bring one back to life. This is why attempting to resuscitate your relationship in any way will do nothing but prove to your ex:

* How easy it is to fuck with you. He can play dead/ghost when he wants, come to life when he wants, and mix every signal imaginable.

* How insecure and dependent you must be.

- How weak you really are.

- That he can count on you to be an ego-boosting, grateful-for-anything, crumb-dependent option.

- That he doesn't have to worry about you meeting a better man.

- *That he won.*

No matter what you've done or haven't done up to this point, none of the above is true, or this book would not be in your hands.

So you have no other choice. You have to accept this death, right? But how can you accept death when there *is* death, but there also isn't?

The only way that a feeling of post-breakup defeat can survive is if you are still in the game, and the opposition seems to be thriving amid your perceived downfall. Death disables defeat from seeping into your psyche because there are no players in the face of death. Death is the ultimate leveler. And even though this is not a game, you still want to win.

So back to the main problem:

How can you accept this death when all you see is your ex LIVING—a much happier life that you can no longer access?

It's easy for friends and family to say, "Things will get better with some distance," "Time heals everything," "You dodged a bullet," "Just turn inward; put yourself first," "Take yourself out on a date!" None of this is applicable, nor does it make any sense right now. In fact, it makes you feel worse. You can't feel hopeful for healing from the passage of time when, right now, you don't feel like you can make it through the next hour. And how are you supposed to turn inward, take yourself out on a date, and put yourself first when you (and all of your best efforts) weren't even good enough for your undeserving ex to put you first?

Breakups are a death that is forever subject to resurrection.

You could move on in the most life-changing ways and still, at any point, even many years down the line…

You get a call or a text from an unknown number that you don't know why, but it looks so familiar. You get an unsolicited update on his status from a mutual friend or from your sister after she ran into his. He pops up in your social media notifications right when you finally start moving on with your life and feeling like yourself again. You may even run into him in a city too big to make any sense of how he's suddenly standing right in front of you.

And just like that, there's one less ex who's six feet under in your relational graveyard.

With toxic exes, in particular, breakups used to ignite a sense of entitlement in me. I assumed all the pain, suffering, and failure was just a rite of passage on my way to the Happily Ever After I had *earned*. It had to be. I was a good person, and even though I struggled with enforcing standards, loving myself, and being a total contradiction, I knew on some level that I was a catch. This pain was just me having to "pay my dues" so I would never take for granted the guy who was going to come along to save me, complete me, and see everything in me that I could not see in myself.

Believing in this eventual return on investment was the only thing that made the pain survivable, but it came at a cost. The cost was my power, self-respect, and the life I was so willing to exchange for a licensed renewal on delusion.

Being a good person who can endure toxic relationships does not entitle you to be saved by a man (whose job should never be to save anyone). Nor does it prevent you from being a doormat in the lives of people who have no problem hijacking yours. Endurance will never attract the life you want, nor will it birth the winner you are about to become—*evolution* will.

But don't think that all you have endured is useless.

Your ability to endure what you have is *proof* that you can *evolve* into The One That Got Away, the winner of this breakup.

If you saw a child who was learning to read and having a hard time pronouncing the words in a book, would you ever say, "Whoa, you better stop. You are *not* a reader. Here, take this coloring book instead"? Of course not. It would destroy the child's ability to believe in a capacity that they had all along. You wouldn't say that because you are confident that with endurance, lessons learned, and evolution as a result of having the sheer courage to *act* on those learned lessons, the child will evolve into a reader. You are living proof of that evolution, or you would not be reading these words right now.

If you can say, without a doubt, that you would never label the child as a colorist and not a reader, stop being a contradiction. Stop minimizing and labeling yourself as the resident colorist whose only purpose is to add color (at the cost of her own) to the colorless lives of shitty people. Start maximizing your ability to act by capitalizing on your *already proven* ability to sense toxicity and endure the kind of pain that is now driving your desire to win instead of defining your downfall.

This shift is not about hardening and becoming cynical. It's about becoming sharper and being able to call your own relational shots. It's about acting on the acceptance of what is beyond resuscitation (your relationship) so that you can rise and reinvent in a way that your ex (and anyone who has ever fucked with you) could never and will never.

It's time to rise above the ashes of *what no longer is* so that you can stop giving life to *what never was* and zero in on exactly *what you are about to kill.*

WHAT NO LONGER IS

* Your relational wardrobe, reading material, and diet. Gone are the rose-colored glasses you wore, the denial you subscribed to, and the crumbs you received.

* Your addiction to the *intensity* of roller coaster, hot/ cold *inconsistency*, and mistaking that for a soulmate connection.

* Your attraction to potential (and allowing that attraction to prevent you from seeing who people are in the present moment).

* Your tolerance for anyone who gets validation by exploiting your hunger for theirs.

WHAT NEVER WAS

- A man who unconditionally loves *himself.*

- A mutual relationship.

- An emotionally intelligent partner. **Emotional intelligence is nonreactivity rooted in *awareness*— self-awareness and awareness *outside of* oneself.** When you are emotionally intelligent, your emotions do not dictate your actions. You are able to take account-ability and be responsible for what you say and do. This is because you have empathy; you can put yourself in other people's shoes. You also know what triggers you so well that you can respond kindly instead of react cheaply. **Toxic people are *clever*. Emotional intelligence requires the denominator of wisdom, which is applied knowledge. Cleverness requires the denominator of an *agenda*, which is applied selfishness.** Your ex is only capable of a self-serving *transaction*ship—not the mutual relationship you claim to want and deserve.

WHAT YOU ARE ABOUT TO KILL

I'm going to share something with you that I struggled with for a long time but felt too ashamed and guilty to admit. Who was I to have these thoughts after a *breakup* when other people were dealing with real pain and real problems? There are so many people who are suffering in this world for all kinds of reasons, but no matter what the situation or who the person is, pain is pain. And we are all entitled to processing ours without simultaneously having to carry the burden of unnecessary guilt for being human.

After one terrible breakup, I didn't want to live anymore. I also couldn't die. The only way I can explain the feeling is that I wanted to end. I didn't know what I wanted to end; I just felt like I needed an ending. And because I was so heartbroken, felt forgotten, and hated who I had become…

I wanted me to end.

But I couldn't kill myself. I was worried about screwing that up too and risking a life where I'd be completely dependent on the family I wanted to make proud—not burdening them. I also worried about other family members who shared many of the same qualities as my ex, whom I was trying to get over and prove wrong.

Looking back, I can now see it was never me that I wanted to kill.

What I really wanted to kill was:

- The pain and powerlessness.

- The insecurity (and subsequent inauthenticity) I had felt since I was a child.

- The weak and unattractive image that my ex had of me (and that I had of myself).

- The desperation.

- The social anxiety that began to border on paranoia. I had a hard time maintaining eye contact with anyone because deep down, I knew how phony I was.

- The need to copy other people's styles, looks, and personalities because I had no style, look, or identity of my own.

- The inadequacy I felt every minute of every day.

- The having to apologize to everyone for every little thing.

- The issues I had with abandonment and the drama I created as a result.

- The jealousy.

- The people-pleasing.

- The mommy and daddy issues.

- The crucifixion I would get for doing what others got a slap on the wrist.

- The chances I gave to people who did not deserve a single one.

- The shame of my bad decisions and how disgusting they made me feel.

- The shame of being lied to and cheated on.

- The shame of *being* a liar and cheating on my intuition by prioritizing my triggers.

- The fear of rejection.

- The need for validation.

- The obsession with what everyone else thought.

- The doormat I had become.

Sometimes we forget that we have *already survived* worse than what we are currently convinced we can't. I was able to kill everything on that list by remembering who the fuck I was—for the first time in my life.

This breakup—including your ex's actions, inactions, and all of the un-dealt with trauma from your past—has you feeling like you are everything on that list. But that list is not who you are.

Do you know who the fuck you are?

> **You are the *owner* of your dysfunctional coping mechanisms, the *awareness* of your ex's bullshit, and the *survivor* of this storm (and many before).**
>
> **You are the one who is finally *acting* on "enough" and has arrived at a place where you can now kill what you need to so that you can rise above as you were born to.**

You are not a light switch, and the disassociation will not happen instantly. But this will get the wheels irreversibly turning. Write your list. Really think about *everything* that you want to kill. Be specific. Cry it out and feel your way through it as you are writing.

When you are done, take a look at it and smile. That list is a direct product of your courage to self-reflect amid heartbreak, fear, and uncertainty—which is something your ex could never do. THAT is who you are. **You are now facing everything that ever scared you into mediocrity and made you feel like you had no choice but to be a victim.**

It's one thing to be ignorant and keep doing the same thing. It's a whole other kind of hell to know better in the moment of not doing better. You know better now. Creating this list has marked the separation between you, *the real you*, and the false identity that being in a relationship with an emotional bum perpetuated.

Once you have your list written, do something to (safely) kill it. Throw it in a contained fire and watch it burn. Those ashes are now your *tailwind*. Your old identity, with all the associated fear and shame, is no longer your headwind. It's dead and gone.

After you burn your list, do something for yourself—even if it doesn't involve leaving your home. Whatever you do, though, do it ceremoniously, just as you would a death, birth, or graduation.

This one is all three.

You are acknowledging the **death** of the man you thought you knew (and everything on your list that made you a sitting duck for this relationship), celebrating the **birth** of who the fuck you *really* are, and honoring your **graduation** from the school of relational amateur hour.

This is your opportunity to build an existence that is brand new and ALL yours, to consciously create every aspect of who you want to become.

My parents conceived me, but Natasha Adamo is a creation of my own drive and imagination. She is a direct result of being fueled by shame to create the person I once never thought I could be, instead of using that shame as a filter to view life and make poor decisions through.

After I killed my list, I wrote down everything I wanted Natasha Adamo to be and do—from the most silly and superficial to the serious and substantial. Some of it stuck, and some didn't; some got edited and revised. It didn't matter. **For the first time in my life, I was actually living—*on* my own terms, *out* of a victim mentality, and *in* the kind of peace that I had finally let all of my dysfunction rest in.**

I know how powerless you feel right now, but you are the furthest thing from powerless. You have *already proven* to have limitless power by continuing to breathe life into everything on that list of yours for all these years. Instead of using this power to your advantage, you've only been able to use it if it meant contributing to your demise and validating a toxic belief system.

This pattern stops right here, right now. You are so much better than what you've allowed yourself to subscribe to, and the bedsores were never worth it. Powerlessness cannot exist without stagnation. And just like physical stagnation will give you painful bedsores, emotional stagnation will create psychological bedsores in the name of everything on your list.

Once you kill your list, you *will* revert back to what's on it. Do not let this get you down, and do not give in. This is a normal, flu-like symptom of the emotional detox you just gave yourself.

Remember, these beliefs have been fused to your identity for so long that they've embedded themselves deep in your neuropathways. It's okay to give yourself some time to adjust. Just don't allow yourself to legitimize resuscitation of what no longer has a pulse— within yourself, your ex, and your relationship.

When someone you love dies, you'll find yourself turning on the street where they live, about to give them a call, or starting to send them a text…until you remember that they're gone, and you can't proceed.

The same goes for everything on your list. When you find yourself reverting to anything on it, you will immediately be reminded that it's dead.

YOU killed it.

You just destroyed everything that nearly destroyed you. And from this point forward, even if you take a few steps back, you are *still ahead* of where you were.

You've risen too high above those ashes to ever go back to square one now.

2

You Will Never Be This Broken Again

Your ex is not the ending point for you. He was a northern star, and you are about to become his karma. Northern stars point you on your way to what is meant for you. They lead you out of bad cycles, into your true self, and toward enforcing standards that attract the kind of relationships and life you deserve. Karma is not revenge, nor is it about bad things happening to terrible people. It's a mirror. Mirrors do not add, subtract, play games, seek validation, or waste time telling people who they are. They simply reflect—just by being *what* they are. If a mirror breaks, the reflection is distorted.

The only way your ex will ever look into a mirror is if it's broken.

Not only does he get to see more of himself in all of the broken pieces, but since there is so much chaos in the reflection, he will never have to come face-to-face with a true and clear reflection of his *own* brokenness. He also gets to remind the mirror of how broken it is, and because of that, how no one else will want to look at it.

Unluckily for him, you are a mirror who is about to unbreak by creating her own certainty right now.

After a breakup, nothing seems certain. Fear of the unknown takes over, and we will do anything to secure a feeling of certainty. Whatever it is that *we know* we can count on, we hold on to it for dear life.

I have sacrificed my own:

- Health

- Sanity

- Values

- Dignity

- Morals

- Reputation

…and self-respect, just to feel one *drop* of the safety that I knew certainty would provide. Even if it was the certainty of my own misery and humiliation! I would create cheap certainty by making weak, unintelligent post-breakup moves that did nothing but strengthen my denial, feed my insecurities, justify impulsive behavior, and translate to my ex that he was better off without me. Everything that resulted in the certainty of my worthlessness was very familiar. It was predictable, and because I *knew* that I could count on that predictability, I had no choice but to embarrassingly latch on.

This is why it's more appealing right now for you to gravitate toward the safety of choosing the well-beaten path of your all-too-familiar pain, self-blame, obsession, and defeat. Whenever you've tried to venture into the uncharted territory of having your own back and acknowledging your worth, the other shoe drops, and you are the fool, every time.

You will never be that fool again. Let's create some real certainty right now.

WHAT YOU CANNOT GUARANTEE:

- You cannot guarantee that you will never get cheated on, lied to, and broken up with ever again.

- You cannot guarantee that your ex will not say and do hurtful, selfish, insensitive, and passive-aggressive things following this breakup—no matter how much you still unconditionally love him.

- You cannot guarantee that your ex's selfish regrets will *ever* evolve into genuine remorse.

- You cannot guarantee that he's learned his lesson.

- You cannot guarantee that you will never break again.

WHAT YOU CAN GUARANTEE RIGHT NOW:

You can guarantee comfort levels.

Although you cannot control what your ex (or what anyone) does or says to you, you can control *how comfortable they feel* doing and saying what they do to you. This all boils down to how willing you are to *act* on the gut feelings that make up your intuition.

I used to think that working on my emotional intelligence would magically rid my world of toxic people. It didn't. The constant letdown of encountering one toxic person after another made it impossible to believe that I was deserving of more. I tried to "love" and "educate" myself into a relational fantasy land and, in the process, wasted years of my life that I will never get back.

> **Regardless of how much you love and protect yourself, toxic people will show up at your door no matter what. They will continue to do so until the end of time. *Even more so* when they pick up on an energy of exclusivity.**

It is human nature to want an "in" to establishments that are just as selective with who is *let* in as they are with the quality in which the property is maintained. Toxic people are obsessed with scoring that "in."

For instance, let's say you owned a prestigious bank. There will be people who know they don't have the money to have an account there but want one anyway because of the ego boost they'll get by association with such an establishment. And because they know that they can't legitimately get an account, they decide they're going to break in and steal your money.

They will do this, all while making you believe that they are interested in (and qualify for) the highest-level account.

Just because you got the best security system money can buy, this does not automatically create a world in which bank robbers not only never enter your bank but cease to exist. **All the security**

system can control is how *comfortable* someone will feel rob-bing your bank when assessing whether or not to rob you.

Do you know when a man says things like, "I've never met anyone I wanted to spend the rest of my life with" or "I don't deserve you," it triggers you into wanting to prove him wrong? When you choose to talk about your proverbial security system (your boundaries, what you will and will not tolerate, etc.), it triggers toxic people into feeling comfortable that they can prove *you* wrong. It translates to them that although you want to *appear* to have a top-notch security system in place, you don't. If your security system were truly legit, you wouldn't need to advertise its legitimacy.

When you make the decision to stop explaining and start *acting* on your security system sounding off, it takes away the one thing toxic people need to fuck with you: their level of comfort.

And now you can guarantee the retrieval of your peace. You can guarantee the comfort that your unconditional love built for them because you are finally prioritizing *yourself*—for the first time in your life.

You can guarantee that you will no longer outsource unconditional love.

Unconditional love is something that has both saved my life and robbed me of one. In movies, songs, television, and fairy tales, those who love unconditionally are viewed as heroes in this world. No matter how poorly these people get treated or how badly they are used, the light of their unconditional love seems to out-mature and outshine the need for healthy limits that only unconditional *self*-love can initiate.

> **Unconditional love is not something that will ever get a toxic person to change. It will only give them something to take advantage of and cash in on when they want.**

I am not opposed to unconditional love. It is the most beautiful and necessary thing in relationships with those who lack a voice and are fully dependent on us. You should unconditionally love your child, your pet, animals, and the one voiceless child who would not be reading these words right now if, at some point, conditions were not put around love that should have been given to her unconditionally: *your younger self.*

In romantic relationships, we are wired to want this more than we realize. I used to require unconditional love in all of my relationships. This was because I never figured out how to deal with the absence of it at an age when putting conditions around the love that was given to me was more damaging than it was educational.

Loving without conditions will distort your sense of reality and take the red out of the flags that are all around you. You will constantly find yourself struggling to figure out whether you're with a soulmate who is "trying his best" to be honest with and value you or a disconnected stranger who only has *his* best interest in mind.

Unconditionally loving others requires that you conditionally love yourself.

Loving people without any kind of healthy limits is not love; it's a lack of *self*-love. You are "loving" without self-protection, self-compassion, and self-awareness.

The only need I used to have was catering to the selfish needs of others. It was, sadly, the only way I could derive a sense of worth; the only way I could have some kind of identity in a life I was living on other people's terms.

Your ex needed unconditional love from you as much as you needed validation from him. It was the only way he could guarantee never having to be accountable or experience any pause in every benefit you provided.

And his validation was the only way *you* could guarantee the denial required to stay in a relationship with him.

With the right man, conditions will never be an issue because they will never be tested. They will be *met* every day—without drama, explanation, or a tactical intention.

When a man unconditionally loves and values *himself,* he will know his own conditions and, therefore, assume you know yours too. This kind of true love between two people *feels* unconditional, but it isn't. It's just that the individual conditions of these two people never have to be introduced. A man who is not toxic will never try to talk you out of your own conditions. He will simply assume that if certain conditions aren't met, he will lose you—just like you'd lose him if you didn't meet his.

Unconditional love is not the same thing as supporting each other through tough times. If you're in a relationship where you both love, honor, and respect each other—in sickness and in health, poverty, and riches, and through the good times and the bad—without any kind of carrot-dangling or tug-of-war drama, that's one of the best things that can happen to you in life. But loving without any kind of conditions in the presence of things like broken trust, abuse, a lack of communication, an absence of honesty, and manipulation is not. It translates as, "I don't deserve more because I know I'll never be more. Please validate me so I can invalidate the pain of a past you don't even care about getting to know. Please show me that my lack of standards will be powerful enough to turn this pile of horse shit into a chest of gold."

True love is not unconditional—it's unselfish and *nonjudgmental*.

This kind of love can be felt and shared on such a deeper, more meaningful, and intimate level because it's protected on both ends by healthy conditions (standards) that are honored by two people who unconditionally love *themselves*.

> **When anyone tells you that they require unconditional love in their romantic relationships, what they're really saying is that they want someone who has no personal limits.**

The most attractive and desirable quality in a partner is unconditional *self*-love. It's when the love and support you have for yourself is so unwavering and self-sufficient that it isn't contingent upon any person or external source doing *anything*. When you unconditionally love yourself, you don't need anyone to give you the sunlight and water you are *already giving yourself*, nor are you interested in watering weeds. If you're interested in someone, it's simply because you *want* to be with them. You don't *need* them to right the wrongs of your past, to be your confidence crutches, or to give you an identity, purpose, and sense of worth. That pressure is gone.

You have been equating that feeling of pressure with passion, a mutual relationship, and a soulmate for way too long. You confused being needed (and ultimately used) with being wanted and cherished because deep down, you did not want or cherish yourself. And you didn't feel worthy of being wanted without having the life's purpose of accommodating to the selfish needs of someone whose egoic meal ticket was your unconditional love.

This is no longer your reality.

I know it's hard to believe, but there is a man out there, right now, who will not only meet you where you've now decided to meet yourself but could shine his shoes with the one you are trying to get over. And you can't claim to want to meet him while simultaneously being and doing everything that would prevent this from happening.

Starting with unconditionally loving everyone but yourself.

You can guarantee that there will no longer be any "degrees."

In past relationships, I was always obsessed with trying to figure out the other person's *degree* of interest and *how much* they were committed to me. The more doom of black and white I sensed, the more I tried to convince myself that it was just another shade of gray. I did this just as much during breakups as I did in my relationships.

Right now, you can guarantee that you will no longer waste time trying to figure out the ever-changing "degrees" to which *anyone* is serious about you, honest with you, committed to you, and in love with you.

Your fears will try everything to complicate this because as long as things are chaotic, you have a license to stay put until you're able to make sense of the nonsensical. The main reason why we continue to investigate degrees post-breakup is that we are addicted to chaos and scared to let go. Chaos is the ultimate enabler. It makes our avoidance of taking out the trash seem righteous (and even courageous) instead of what it really is: you being an emotional hoarder, volunteering to be kept in a mediocrity chokehold.

There's no need to complicate *any* of the relationships in your life. You are either being respected and communicated with, or you're not. He's either self-aware and capable of a mutual relationship, or he's not. Things like emotional intelligence, honesty, respect, and communication are not qualities that can ever be partly or halfway there. There's no need to open an investigation or wonder if you'll get "more" of something that's either there or it's not.

And now you can guarantee your ability to recognize and act on THAT.

You can guarantee all consequences and no access.

Everything in life has a consequence. If your ex dishonored you, lied to you, was inconsistent, and made you feel like you were hard to love, the real consequence will never be your endless explanations and empty threats.

It will be losing any and ALL access to you.

When your ex decided to do what he did, he lost the benefit of having you in his life. Taking the time to explain to him what he lost is not only pointless, it's humiliating.

Not everyone can afford the privilege and luxury of having you *as a friend*, let alone a partner in a romantic relationship.

And now you can guarantee that you will no longer be picking up the tab.

You can guarantee that you will never, ever be this broken again.

You are the only person in this world who can ensure that you will not only survive this breakup but that you will THRIVE as a result of growth through survival. No one else can make this happen, so stop depending on your ex. He needs you to keep believing that he is the end-all, be-all because the moment you realize that it has always and will always be YOU...

That is the moment his reign ends, and a life he never thought you were capable of begins.

YOU are the only one who can guarantee this WIN.

YOU are the only one who can dictate your worth.

YOU are the only person who, for *every day* of your life, will be there with and for you through *everything*.

It will be YOU who will inevitably break again, yes, but never like this. And you can find meaning and gratitude in this particular break.

It broke you open enough to realize that you have had enough. It broke you open enough to want more for yourself and your life. It broke you open enough to believe that in the face of defeat, you can rise up, reinvent, and win this breakup because you can. It broke you open enough for us to find each other. And now...

You have unbroken *yourself* by creating the certainty we just did.

3

Everything You Want Is on Your White Horse

You have been undervalued in relationships your entire life because all you have known is to undervalue yourself. And no matter how angry you become or how much better you think you deserve, you will continue to be undervalued if you do not understand this:

> Winning your breakup is not defined by how much you can temporarily trigger and unglue your ex. Any amateur with a social media account can do that. Winning your breakup comes from how you *choose to proceed* when experiencing any situation that makes you *feel* the most triggered and unglued.

You were born with a power that is more attention commanding than a "perfect" body, clear skin, an Ivy League education, and money in the bank. When owned and activated, this power is life changing. Instead of triggering your ex, it will have him questioning reality as he knows it. And it will award you with the kind of confidence that is not contingent upon a purchase made or a person not leaving you.

You can activate this power of yours at any time and use it to *win* —**without reducing anything to a game.**

The only reason you haven't done this is not because you're weak. It's because you've allowed your heart to hold your intuition hostage, which has prevented you from acting on it. And if you can't act on your intuition, you will only be able to operate within the prison cell of reactivity.

I get it, though. You can't take it anymore. Every morning, you wake up to the nightmare of "He hasn't reached out. It really *is* over. He's back to being the guy he was in the beginning, and now, he's with someone who's everything I'm not. He gained another follower on social media, and I'm not even worth a call. What is he doing? I need to know!" You are convinced that an answer from him will set you free, but a knife will never be a Band-Aid. And because you're an emotional cutter, you react. *To everything.*

THIS IS WHERE YOUR WHITE HORSE COMES IN.

The hardest thing to do after a breakup (and in life) is staying on your White Horse. The White Horse and I were not always as close as we are today. I used to think that the White Horse was stupid, a guaranteed way to ensure I'd be forgotten.

It all started after I found out my boyfriend at the time had been cheating on me with someone I considered a friend. I wanted to frame them, catch them in the act, call them both out on their lies, and destroy their reputations. I basically wanted to make them feel as much pain and humiliation as I did.

Just as I picked up the phone to call him and get the plan in motion, my Mom called. The moment I heard her voice, I broke down. "You've got to stay on your White Horse," she said. And thanks to her explaining this concept that she came up with years ago, I went from feeling completely out of control that night to deciding to cut them both off—for good. I sent a short and respectful text to him explaining that I was done and to please leave me alone. I didn't respond to any of his replies, nor did I mention what I knew. This wasn't about being the "gotcha!" police or playing games. It was, for once, about *me*—retaining my mental health, prioritizing my peace, and making a clean break.

When mutual friends asked what was going on, I explained that I was done with him. Period. They were so taken back by how classy, private, in control, and indifferent I behaved that many said it inspired them to take action in their own lives. This inspired me to keep going. I never once gossiped or said anything negative about him; I didn't say anything at all. Behind every closed door, I broke down. But outside of those doors, I did the best I could to live life. My Mom kept reminding me that I didn't owe anyone an explanation. The only thing I did owe was an apology to myself for allowing my emotions to dictate my actions for so long.

After a few weeks, I had made so much progress that I became more protective of that progress than I was interested in reacting to stupidity. The cost had become too high. I realized that reacting wouldn't change anything other than my level of self-respect. It wouldn't make my ex regret what he did and miraculously start to respect me, nor would it make me begin to respect myself. There was no point in trying to get him to understand where I was coming from or how I felt. His actions had *already proven* that he was incapable of thinking about anyone but himself.

Reacting had now become a liability instead of an involuntary reflex.

In the end, my ex and ex-friend both ended up calling so much that I had no choice but to block them. Everyone eventually caught onto what they did. They both destroyed their reputations, lost friends, and had a big, dramatic falling out. I felt embarrassed for them. And this was all without me doing anything except stay on my White Horse. It was like the universe took care of them for me once I met it halfway and proved my emotional intelligence.

OUR WHITE HORSE IS EMOTIONAL INTELLIGENCE.

A Knight in Shining Armor is widely known as someone who comes to the aid of another. In fairy tales, the Knight in Shining Armor rides in on his White Horse against all odds. He rescues the damsel in distress, and all is right with the world. They ride off into the sunset of their own Happily Ever After and never look back.

Have you ever noticed how that knight doesn't get off his horse? How he stays focused on his goal and never wavers in his decision and disposition—no matter what anyone else says or does?

You need to be your own Knight in Shining Armor. Be the class act that everyone is in awe of instead of the lunatic who needs a muzzle and a leash.

When you see or hear something that triggers you, exhibit some grace under pressure. Stay on your White Horse when all you want to do is retaliate and react.

Nonreactivity is the fastest way to activate your personal power and command respect. Toxic people can never fuck with those who don't react to their theatrics.

When it comes to breakups, it's easy to get stuck in this vicious cycle of plotting our upcoming "revenge" and then getting stuck in the mud of unnecessary guilt, obsessing over everything that's already happened. We do this because the heartbreak of the present moment is so painful that we're scared that if we fully feel it, we won't make it out alive.

No matter what, all roads of this cycle end with *blaming ourselves* for our ex's behavior. We do this in our minds, with friends and family—all while stalking our ex on social media, trying to find more to uncover and obsess over. We look for validation from any source that will allow us to go over every detail until we exhaust ourselves and everyone around us.

And when emotional exhaustion kicks in, reactivity (getting off our White Horse) feels like our only option.

Yes, it's important to take responsibility for what you did wrong in your relationship. Just like relationships take two people, so do breakups. But being in complete denial of what your ex consistently did, focusing only on the good parts, and blaming yourself for everything bad will accomplish nothing. It'll just make you that much more prone to getting off your White Horse and reacting.

The lies, disrespect, and manipulation you were on the receiving end of WERE NOT FAKE; you are not hallucinating here. You didn't just wake up one morning and decide to feel like shit because you were being treated so incredibly.

There is no longer a need to question what *you know* you've seen, heard, and felt—just so you can keep pedestaling a man who you not only *know* is a total dead end but whose behavior made you de-pedestal *yourself*.

It's okay to take responsibility for allowing your fear of abandonment to facilitate turning a blind eye. But you should never take responsibility for someone hating themselves so much that they had no other option than to get you to question your worth.

How they treat you is not how they feel about you. How they treat you is how they feel about *themselves*.

I've worked with so many people over the years who have asked, "What if my ex moves on to someone better? What if they *become* someone better?"

The connection we fail to make is that un-dealt with trauma (and the low self-esteem it breeds) wires us to put a premium on potential. We become attracted (and subsequently attached) to *what could be*. This prevents us from seeing and accepting who someone *has proven themselves to be* in the present moment. Because of this, we are able to insert value and meaning into any hint of potential—even when we know it's not good for our mental health. This denial of our own reality allows us to excuse and ignore the red flags further—no matter how obvious they are.

Getting on your White Horse allows you to plug back into reality and be above the bullshit, reevaluate your relationship, and examine your part in what took place. You can then choose how you want to *respond* to a situation instead of bouncing from one drama to the next.

If you're ever in doubt about what to do when you get triggered and want to get off your White Horse, picture yourself watching the story of your life in a movie theater with me.

Now imagine we've gotten to the point in your life story that you're at today.

What would you be cheering yourself on to do?

Would you be throwing popcorn at the screen, yelling, "You BETTER keep contacting him! You need to explain yourself more. Don't listen to Natasha. Text him and see if he wants to talk. Get drunk and send him a tit pic! Post a desperate selfie, an obvious quote, and then stalk his Mom and cousin on social media for a few more hours. Stop trying to preserve your dignity! Reach out to his new girlfriend and tell her how bad he is in bed."

No, you would not be doing that. We would both be rooting you on—to hit your limit of being fucked with, take action, and *win*.

The best movies have dynamic characters. These people are uncommon among the commoners. They observe more than they invest, act more than they speak, and enjoy their own company more than they care about popularity.

There is nothing in this world like watching a dynamic character. Very rarely do you get to witness someone whose actions you have no choice but to listen to because they speak so clearly for themselves. Think of the main character in your favorite movie. I guarantee you it is a dynamic one.

A dynamic character is a person whom everyone wants to:

* Be with

* Be like

* Wish they had never fucked with

No one wants to watch the main character go gossip to others, throw a tantrum, piss their pants, and waste their time. They don't want to watch the main character lose their power trying to get a "win-win" with an opponent who *disqualified themselves* just by being who they are.

They want to watch the underdog get up after being knocked to the ground and _crush_ their opponent. The more dignifiedly they crush them, the rarer and more impressive they are.

Most people don't realize that if someone has the capacity to devalue you, their ego _needs_ you to react by trying to immaturely retaliate and devalue them back. But when you can totally annihilate them without disembarking from the dignity, self-love, and standards they tried to rob you of, _that's_ real power.

THIS IS WHY ALL DYNAMIC CHARACTERS HAVE A WHITE HORSE.

It can be very lonely on your White Horse, though. After all, there's only room for one. But remember, being alone is not a symptom of worthlessness, nor is it a definition of how forgettable you are. It's proof that you prioritize your peace over your insecurities and fears. It's evidence that you're not a doormat, and it is confirmation that outside validation is not needed.

Your ex would rather end it with you, _not_ because you are not enough, but because working things out would require him to have emotional intelligence that he just doesn't have. Do not let your insecurities confuse you here. There are no riches that he was actively withholding and now flaunting for real on social media. He is empathetically bankrupt and incapable of stepping up in the way you deserve. Remember, empathy is nothing more than the ability to put yourself in other people's shoes. The only shoes your ex will ever be able to put himself in are his own.

And you are no longer the doormat.

You are the White Horse, the rider, and the ride into your own Happily Ever After.

A reader of mine shared with me how she stays on her White Horse: "Whenever I see something that triggers me and makes me want to reach out to my ex, I get on my White Horse and find dignity. I close my eyes and imagine a warrior woman—a radiant, beautiful, strong version of myself—the version I always wanted to be—on a White Horse. This woman scoops up the heartbroken, beaten, and weak version of me from the base of a tree in a dark wood. She carries me with her as we gallop off to my own mind palace, replete with a fireplace, warm bath, stacks of books, heavy blankets, and nourishing food. During the ride, I melt into this warrior woman and use her strong-rooted, steady legs to find solace in this place of nonreactivity—as I am able to ride past the bullshit and into my power."

Toxic people realize the shackles they are in when they see you break free from your own. When your ex senses that you are happy, succeeding, moving on, and having the courage to be and do what he can't, his inferiority complex will be triggered, This is due to his own lack of self-awareness, emotional intelligence, and self-love.

And rather than take a hint to self-reflect and look in the mirror, he will try to yank your chain passively, manipulate you, reaction-monger, and bust your boundaries. Keep going. Do not give in and do not react to anything—*even his silence*. **Your reactivity is caviar to his ego.** It takes someone with real power and strength to remain calm, communicate through her actions that she can't be sunk, and move the fuck on.

> **Reacting to your ex in any way translates that you are more comfortable being an option to him than you are being the only option to *yourself*.**

You can be completely out of control in your head, in your heart, and when you're breaking down in the bathroom at work. But to anyone who disrespected you and has an expectation that you are going to behave a certain way, *surprise them*.

You don't build self-respect by trying to control the uncontrollable. You build self-respect by taking complete ownership of what you *do* have control over and surrendering to what you do not. You may not be able to control your emotions right now, but you can control how you *react* to those emotions. Remember, no one can "make you" react. The only person who can make you react or respond is *yourself*.

* Response is rooted in action.

* Reactivity is rooted in un-dealt with trauma and feeling the need to prove worth you don't really believe you have.

Be remembered in your own fairy tale as The One That Got Away because she actually *stayed* away, remained on her White Horse, and handled her shit with dignity. The only way to educate the ignorant is by taking action that they are incapable of taking. Your words (wasted on them) will just make you look ignorant (and feel powerless).

Whenever I'm in pain, I notice that I'll default to taking responsibility for other people's behavior. It's the only way I can maintain a sense of control when everything feels out of control. It took me years to realize that the behavior of others is a GIFT. It's a window into *their* pain and *their* issues; it has nothing to do with you. I was able to remain on my White Horse when I realized that what my ex said and did was coming from a place of *his own* insecurities and egoic thirst. The only reason his behavior activated me was because *I was* giving life to *my own* insecurities and egoic thirst—not him.

No one can come along and activate anything that you are not actively giving life.

You know how you can put your phone on Do Not Disturb? The same thing can be done for anyone or anything that makes you feel like shit. When your phone is on Do Not Disturb, it doesn't "block out" calls, texts, emails, and alerts. It just doesn't react to them in a way that would distract or derail you. You don't need to waste time trying to "block out" your ex's toxicity. Just make yourself unavailable to it by not reacting.

Make the decision with me right now to go into Do Not Disturb. Let's be unavailable to our triggers so that we can be more available to our White Horse and set boundaries that will give us the standards we deserve.

4

Set Boundaries, Enforce Standards, and Never Negotiate

What's the difference between a person everyone wants to know and a person everyone knows they can use?

Boundaries.

When it comes to mainstream breakup advice, there's a big emphasis on reintroducing yourself to the world by raising your standards after getting screwed over. This pumps people up and motivates them into a take-no-prisoners approach when it comes to respect, but it never lasts. It's like getting excited to build a mansion on quicksand or realizing the freedom money can allow you but never being taught how to earn and invest it. A solid foundation will give you the opportunity to build your dream home. Knowing how to make and save money will give you the chance to earn and invest wisely.

The same logic applies when it comes to having standards.

If you find that your standards always get lost in the moment, that you're constantly reminding yourself to "keep your standards high," it's because there are no boundaries backing them up. **Boundaries are what *give you* standards that no one can negotiate down.** They are what protect you from being manipulated, used, and abused.

Standards are a *symptom* of healthy boundaries. They are your minimum relational requirements, the qualities that need to be present in order for you to allow access to all the *value* that your boundaries protect and preserve. When your standards are not met, that should be known as a "deal breaker." Unfortunately, it has become a signal for you to wonder, "What did I do wrong? There must be something wrong with *me*, or else he'd meet me at the standard I set. I need to try harder."

Standards cannot exist without boundaries backing them up. Boundaries are a recognition of value. Standards are the criteria that need to be met *in order for that value to be accessed*. If you don't believe that you have any value as a human being, you'll never feel like you have anything to protect and preserve. You'll also feel guilty and stupid for trying to protect something that you don't truly believe is worthwhile (yourself). Everything will be up for grabs. This is why it's essential to recognize your value and set boundaries accordingly.

Without setting boundaries, you will have no standards to enforce, no self to love, and no relationship that is ever healthy, mutual, and drama-free.

Everything that you are feeling and experiencing right now is a direct result of three things:

1. Decisions you've made based on what you've chosen to tolerate.

2. Allowing those tolerations to define your "boundaries."

3. Never enforcing standards (that you know you should) because those "boundaries" are not boundaries. They're just another way to enable denial and evade the truth.

Boundaries are whatever your limits are with regard to how others treat you. They are what make you the C.E.O. of YOU. And as C.E.O., *you* are the one who gets to decide the structure of your entity. You are the one who dictates the limits, laws, and ethics as far as what is and what is not acceptable.

Boundaries teach people how to treat you. They also teach you how to treat yourself. You now have limits on how you *respond* to your line being crossed—whether it's someone else crossing that line or the cynical audience in your own head.

Many people love the idea of being an entrepreneur. Still, they resort to forever talking about their dreams, posting entrepreneurial quotes, and never finding a way out of answering to a boss who does not appreciate them and a job that does not fulfill them. Although not everyone wants to be a successful entrepreneur, I think it's safe to say that successful entrepreneurs are respected. The same goes in the relational world, except in the relational world, the *only* truly respected people are the emotional entrepreneurs. Implementing boundaries after a breakup with a toxic ex is the ultimate emotional entrepreneurial move.

One of my favorite quotes explains it perfectly:

> *"Entrepreneurship is living a*
> *few years of your life like most people won't,*
> *so that you can spend the rest of your*
> *life like most people can't."*
>
> —Student (unidentified) of Warren G. Tracy

It is now time to live your post-breakup life like most people won't (with boundaries) so that you can spend the rest of your emotional and relational life like most people can't—not dependent on outside validation.

Boundaries are what checkmates your ex's view of you from "in need of employment" to C.E.O.—the C.E.O. who has suddenly eclipsed *them* and their bullshit. This is the fastest, most effective way to reintroduce your ex to who the fuck you are. You communicate through dignified action that you are done.

You are done taking him more seriously than he takes himself.

You are done holding him to a higher standard than he holds himself to.

And now you are able to hold *yourself* to the standard you've always needed to.

Your ex may have demoted you from your ever-changing position in the shady "business" he runs, but guess what? Your boundaries just bolted the door of the *Fortune* 500 company that *you* are now the C.E.O. of. Bravo!

Boundaries are as solid as they are uncomplicated. Explaining them to others does not activate them, apologies from others do not deactivate them, and an orgasm does not make them negotiable. They do not operate on a case-by-case basis.

Your ex got away with things that you were not okay with, but you unconditionally loved him and let it slide. Instead of recognizing your commitment to him and willingness to move forward, he took this as a sign that he could bust your boundaries further because you didn't unconditionally love yourself. He could get all the benefits of having a committed, monogamous, loyal, and honest partner without having to give any of the same commitment, monogamy, loyalty, and honesty in return.

And even though it is true that people will lose respect for you when they see that you clearly do not respect yourself, people who are not toxic will never try to exploit their observation. They will lose attraction, communicate clearly, honor their *own* boundaries, and move on.

Actions speak louder than words, but *patterns* speak louder than actions. Your ex could tell from your patterns that you clearly didn't value yourself enough to have limits. If you did, there's no way you'd still be seeking closure, explaining how you feel, and going on about what needs to change.

You would be done and gone.

Does your ex try to negotiate with the Gas and Electric company every month? No. He makes sure that he pays his bills on time because he knows that there won't be any hot water or electricity if he doesn't. Does this make him a better man? No. It just makes the

Gas and Electric company an entity that is protected, valued, and not to be negotiated with. You either respect their limits and get to experience the *value* they provide for your household, or you don't.

Boundaries are not something that is ever going to make a toxic person nontoxic. They should never be implemented as a threat, an ultimatum, or a scare tactic—only as a calm, unwavering guide (just like the Gas and Electric bill).

If you're still trying to make sense of your ex's bullshit, his mixed signals, and hurtful behavior, it's because you don't believe you have any worth beyond a relationship with him. If you could not implement boundaries in your relationship with him, it's because you don't feel like you have basic value as a human being. You don't believe that you matter enough to have a limit. And you don't believe that his actions could ever be a result of his own self-hatred—only a spotlight on your lack of worth.

There's nothing you can do to change what you tolerated in the past and how it made you look. But you *can* change the way your ex views you now. Toxic people have a very short relational memory. They'll remember you as the same person you were in the past *as long as it continues* to line up with who you are, what you do, and who you present yourself to be today. Don't worry if there's no way for him actually to see the changes you're making. It's amazing the kind of curiosity and insecurity that silence, minding your own business, and realizing your worth can ignite.

Your ex did what he did to you because *he could*—not because you couldn't be enough. **The fact that you tolerated and excused everything he did was not an act of true love—it was a result of un-dealt with trauma, a fear of abandonment, and not believing that you had any basic value.** True love is not what makes us blind to the red flags. A lack of self-worth is what blinds us. At the very least, you need to know that you have value as a person on this planet. If you don't, you will never be able to implement boundaries without complication and guilt.

Boundaries are simple and straightforward. If they seem impossible to execute, it's because you are a people-pleaser who was never given a chance to learn how to love herself unconditionally. To those who can, at the very least, recognize that they have basic value, boundaries will *naturally* and *involuntarily* be set and acted upon.

The best part about boundaries is that you (and only you) get to decide what your limits are. The hardest part is maintaining them around family, friends, and an ex who will make you feel guilty for not making "special adjustments." Some will even call you crazy when they realize that they can no longer manipulate you. They'll remind you of your bond, your history, how sorry they are…whatever they can to tear down your walls.

Others will view your boundaries as a "red flag" and try to make you feel mean and immature for having them. I've had many people in my life interpret my boundaries as me holding on to resentment and being unable to maturely "let things go" when really, I don't have any ill will. All I did was cut off the access that they once had to me. It's crazy when you realize just how many people relied on you hating yourself enough to confuse their toxicity with true love, empathy, and concern—*just so they could feel significant* and in control.

If you are in a toxic relationship . . .

Loving yourself, having your own back, and setting nonnegotiable boundaries with enforced standards will *always* be a threat to your partner—no matter how much of a "champion" they pretend to be for you.

If your ex has a problem with you recognizing your value enough to have actual limits, if he has a problem with you wanting to be treated with decency and respect, it really is *his* problem, not yours. Stop trying to make it your problem.

Boundaries are not something that ever need to be justified or explained. I am all for respectfully communicating *one time* that a boundary has been crossed. But explaining your boundaries to someone who has consistently proven that they cannot do anything but bust them is a bad idea. Having to teach a grown man the emotional ABCs and explain why something hurtful and disrespectful was, indeed, hurtful and disrespectful is not sexy.

Since when did it become your duty to emotionally potty train grown adults? **In life, you have to understand that some people will piss on your proverbial rug.** Whether it's on social media, with friends, family, a romantic partner, or in business, it has nothing to do with you. If a grown, healthy adult came into your beautiful home and peed in the middle of your living room on the carpet, what would you do? Would you cry and say, "*Oh, gee. Is my home so awful looking* that this poor person assumed it didn't have a bathroom? *Am I so awful* that they didn't feel like they could ask me where the bathroom was? I should try to explain to them that this is the wrong thing to do, shouldn't I?" Hell no. You would escort the un-potty-trained adult OUT of your home and not tie your value to them pissing their pants!

> **I know you feel like you have no choice but to internalize your ex's disrespectful behavior. As a result, you feel like you have to *explain* to him how much he hurt you and busted your boundaries.**

> **This is because your heart wants him to validate your pain more than your dignity wants to have to act on the pain he caused.**

When you allow a toxic ex to come in and out of your life and continue to use you like his personal doormat, he's not going to arrive at the realization that "this incredible, one-of-a-kind woman is never able to enforce the standards she keeps explaining to me she has. It's such a turn-on! I couldn't have more respect for how she carries herself. After manipulating her, lying to her, flirting with other girls, breaking up with her, making her feel guilty, and ghosting for a month, she still answers my texts and takes the time to explain what I did 'wrong.' I've hit the jackpot! Her love for me is limitless. And she's so committed to me that she has no problem with me not being committed to her! I need to apologize for everything I did and commit right now before I lose this once-in-a-lifetime gem.'"

Instead, he will get an ego inflation like you cannot believe. He'll think (and most likely tell his family and friends), "WHOA. She really is *that* desperate, and I'm *that* powerful, irreplaceable, and in control. I can do whatever the hell I want and get away with it. She's got major issues, not me. If what I did was *that* bad, there's no way I'd still be getting all this access. Now I know that I can go out and find better than her *but still use her as a backup*. Life is good!"

There's so much out there with regard to what healthy boundaries are, how to implement them, and what to do with them once implemented. This can run the risk of making people more reliant on a formula than a feeling. Clients often ask me how boundaries are supposed to *feel*, especially after a breakup.

Here's what healthy boundaries feel like:

* I don't need anyone or anything to complete me. I am enough—just as I was and just as I am.

- I will lose any relationship before I get off my White Horse and lose *myself*.

- I have every right to feel the way I feel and respond in dignified action (not triggered reactivity).

- It's not my job to apologize and comfort other people when they have an allergic and victimized reaction to my limits. People who recognize their own value enough to *believe* that that value needs to be protected by healthy boundaries will never resent me for loving myself enough to do the same.

- It's not my job to make people love and choose me. It's my job to love and choose myself.

- Saying no feels incredible. I don't feel guilty anymore.

- It's okay if people criticize me, don't agree with me, or get upset. They are entitled to their feelings as much as I am entitled to mine.

- If I'm crazy-labeled because I can't be manipulated, so be it.

- Whether someone treats me with respect is not contingent upon my value or the level to which I cater to their needs.

- Red flags are no longer an investigation opener. They are an *action initiator.* I now walk away from bullshit, and it feels great.

- People will treat me the way I allow myself to be treated.

- If anyone shows me through their actions that they can't respect me, be honest with me, or see my value, I no longer try to get them to make better decisions. I know my worth.

- It should never take someone losing me to value me.

Stop trying to qualify yourself for a man who has *already disqualified himself* with lies, inconsistency, and shady behavior.

Stop arguing with what is, just so you have a license to keep your "boundaries" negotiable and settle for less than what *you know* you deserve.

Stop blaming *yourself* for *your ex's inability* to be decent, honest, consistent, and humane.

You are not beneath him. This *mentality* is beneath YOU.

YOU CAN LET GO of the *idea* of a man who contradicts everything he has proven to be in reality.

YOU CAN ACCEPT WHAT IS. Just like you have the right to define who you are through your own decisions, patterns, actions, and words, your ex has the right to define himself! Do not take that away from him. Step aside and become more observant than you are invested in making everything fill your self-fulfilling prophecy of "I am not enough." And just because your ex's definition of *himself* is painful to accept, that doesn't mean you allow it to define who *you* are.

YOU CAN BELIEVE that you matter enough to have a limit.

And when you do, you'll always be able to put your mental health first without succumbing to guilt.

You are reading this because you have consistently found yourself devalued and disrespected. It is now time to let your boundaries take out the trash and allow your standards to ensure that it *stays* out. I am not literally calling your ex "trash" in a hateful way, and I don't mean to offend anyone here. I personally define trash as anything that is not needed, not useful, and toxic to *your* household.

The man and relationship you're trying to get over are all three of those things.

Setting boundaries and enforcing standards is something that no one else can do for you. For the rest of your life, people will either exploit the doormat you are or be turned off by your lack of boundaries. Plain and simple.

Nothing will make you feel more loved and validated than having the courage to *act* on your line being crossed. Having access to you and your heart is a *privilege*—not something that a man who only has crumbs to offer, a selfish agenda to fill, and jealousy to ignite gets the red carpet rolled out for.

You've always been worth more than what you've tolerated. It is now time to prove it to yourself once and for all.

5

The Key to Unconditional Confidence and Self-Love

You have spent your whole life looking for people to see in you what you do not see in yourself. You cannot see these things in yourself because in your childhood, you were made to feel defective by someone you loved, looked up to, relied on, and trusted. This could be very easy to identify or extremely subtle and more difficult to recognize. It could have come from your Mom, Dad, a parental figure, a peer, or a teacher. They made you feel like you had to work for things that no child should ever have to work for (love, approval, support, acceptance, encouragement, respect, etc.), which wounded you. Your solution became people-pleasing, trying to be perfect for them at the expense of your emotional development.

Many people (consciously and subconsciously) have children because they know a child will give them the unconditional love that they cannot find in their relationship, from the world, and within themselves. You were not put on this planet to be an unconditional love ATM or a marriage savior. You did not come down from the sky, open your parents' legs, and say, "Make me. I'm ready!" Your parents brought you into this world. And no matter how old you are, you will always be their child.

You tried your hardest to be who they needed you to be—not because you had anything to prove, you were already more than enough, but so they could feel better about their own perceived defectiveness. And because they never could, neither could you. This breakup has reopened that same wound—a wound you have been subconsciously picking the scab of (through toxic relationships) every time a new one forms.

As a child, you needed unconditional love from your parents. But if they were not able to love themselves unconditionally, you were never able to receive unconditional love and learn how to activate it from within. As a result, your emotional survival became dependent on *validation*—from your parents, family, and community. No matter what these people did or did not do, you unconditionally loved them. It was the only way that your little developing heart and brain could cope with an absence of something you did not yet have the tools to identify.

Children are voiceless, defenseless, and reliant on the emotional and physical care that needs to be given to them. Without it, they cannot survive. These people let you believe that you had to work for their validation and love because if you ever stopped working for it, they would have to come face-to-face with where they went wrong in their own lives. They would have to employ courage they did not know how to jump-start and kill the kind of dysfunction within themselves that you already did in Chapter 1.

Having to work for basic emotional necessities was all you knew as a child, which is why you didn't see it as problematic. It was also the only thing you had to stay alive—both physically and emotionally. It's not like you could break up with your family, switch schools, make your own money, and take care of yourself.

You are now an adult whose toxic relational dynamics have become habitual. You have turned to partners that take you for granted, jealous family members, disloyal friends, and ungrateful coworkers. You may have even turned to substances, social media, or superficial purchases to elicit feelings you've never been able to activate from within because of this un-dealt with trauma. You can't trust your own eyes and ears unless someone validates what you *already know* you have seen and heard.

You keep trying to be "The One" that's "good enough" to "complete" other people because that's exactly what you want from the outside world: *completion*.

If this works (it never does), you will then feel like you have the kind of worth that you were never given a chance to realize you've had all along.

You have continued to love yourself conditionally because that's exactly what you got as a child from the people whose unconditional love you were the hungriest for. Because of this, you are now an adult who is unable to let other people own their own behavior. You still internalize the hurtful behavior of others just like you did as a voiceless child. You've never known any different.

Your entire sense of worth is dependent on everything outside of your control, everything outside of *yourself*. This is why you feel like you need closure from your ex before you can move on. **What you've *already witnessed* is not enough. It doesn't "count" unless the man who was heartless enough to do what he did becomes empathetic enough to be able to admit that what he did was heartless.** This makes absolutely no sense.

The only person who can stop you from winning this breakup is **you,** not your ex. Yes, he is your "opponent" in this breakup. But first, you need to address the opponent staring back at you in the mirror and get on the same team as her, or you will never have a life to call your own.

This is not about being a victim, nor is it about vilifying and casting blame on your parents or anyone in your childhood.

Your parents did the best they could.

No one had the perfect parents, no one will be the perfect parent, and anyone can procreate regardless of emotional intelligence, self-awareness, and mental health. This is about realizing that you now have another option. It may feel like you're destined to be a toxicity magnet, but you no longer have to make relational decisions based on the shame of being emotionally orphaned as a child.

You now have the ability to *walk away*.

A woman I know, who is far wiser and more successful than me, once said, "You know what the difference between successful and unsuccessful people is, Natasha? The ability to walk away." She then went on to say how unsuccessful people keep going back and kicking around the same ideas, issues, toxic relationships, fake friendships, etc., and then wonder why they come out with the same garbage in the end. She explained that truly successful people are in it for the long haul, but they also recognize when to get the fuck out of Dodge. And she was right.

For most of my life, self-love meant spray tans and manicures, gainful employment, lots of fake friends, being in a relationship, having a gym membership, and pleasing others. I had to rely on the superficial to define my self-love because if I looked at the substantial, it told an even more pathetic story.

If you want to know exactly how much value someone believes they have, take a look at:

- What they tolerate (in themselves and with others).

- How they deal with milestones, success, and good news (their own and other people's).

- How they deal with failure, abandonment, rejection, and bad news (their own and other people's).

- How quick they are to ACT on red flags versus how quick they are to open an "investigation" (that they cannot emotionally afford).

- The kind of people that they gravitate to and work extra hard to please.

- How much they care about what other people think.

- How well they treat those who can do nothing for them.

- What they find important and unimportant (in society, themselves, and others).

- What they find attractive and unattractive (in themselves and others).

- Whether they try to take ownership of and internalize the behavior of others.

- Their need to explain versus their ability to *respond* (through dignified action).

- Whether they will ACT on their standards not being met, their boundaries being busted, and *get away* from what they know is not good for their mental health.

Self-love is not only reserved for the "lucky, popular, and beautiful" people. It's about recognizing your value as a human being and having your own back as a result of that recognition. It's about gaining confidence from being okay with losing anyone or anything before you lose your mental health. It's about understanding that anyone who makes you feel worthless does so because they cannot tap into their own worth.

If a man who doormats and manipulates you is unable to doormat and manipulate another woman, it's not because of her bigger boobs, prettier face, better hair, success, or whatever you think she has that you don't. The one commonality in the most desirable and unfuckwithable women is having an emotional life of their own. And the only thing that can give you that is *boundaries*—actual limits that are not subject to negotiation—*and standards that enforce those limits*. Even when these women struggle with feelings of insecurity (as we ALL do), they refuse to put up with their emotional intelligence being insulted. **And when this becomes habitual, the love that they have for themselves stops becoming conditional.**

When you love yourself unconditionally, you can create your own sense of safety in life instead of needing romantic partners to do it for you. And you automatically become the most beautiful person in the room.

Winning a genetic lottery takes no effort. Committing to yourself in a social media world that is committed to tearing your confidence down, getting behind yourself *after* a relationship with a toxic partner who was committed to nothing other than feeding his ego… THAT is where true beauty begins. Beauty that even toxic people can "respect" and "appreciate" enough to realize that they are in the presence of someone who eclipses them in every way.

Even if you don't take the best care of your body right now, you'd never go into a building where *you knew* there were cancer-causing chemicals. And you'd never feel guilty or continue to beat yourself up for years about not going into that building, *right?*

So why continue to expose yourself to the metaphorical cancer that toxic people are and then *feel bad* about protecting your own *mental* health?

When you have a high-quality relationship with yourself, you'll stop experiencing guilt paralysis for having boundaries in low-quality relationships.

The hard part is not self-love. You came into this world loving yourself and thinking that you were more than enough. The hard part is having to cut through all of the hate that has accumulated for the adult you've become.

At the lowest points in my life, the only thing that would get me out of my depression was advocating for someone who was voiceless and defenseless. I could relate to them so well. If a child, an animal, or an older adult needed help, I didn't have to think about it. I just took immediate action.

Sometimes it takes getting out of your own head and saving someone (who feels just as voiceless and defenseless) for you to finally save yourself.

In one of my favorite movies, *It's a Wonderful Life*, George Bailey is about to end his life by jumping off a bridge. Clarence, his guardian angel, knows that the only way to save George is by turning into human form, diving into the river, and calling for help. He knows that George will forget about committing suicide and save him. That, in turn, saves George's life.

> **Someone is drowning in the river right now who does not know how to swim. She needs you to drop everything and help her. As a thank-you for saving her life and loving her unconditionally, she will prove to you that you can win this breakup, make your ex regret what he did, and act on boundaries that you have felt too guilty to uphold in the past.**

I want you to find a photo of yourself when you are under six years old. Find one where you are at your happiest and most carefree. After you choose your photo, go somewhere you can have some privacy (even if it's in your parked car, it doesn't matter). Now get that photo out and take a good look at that little girl. All she wants is to be accepted and loved.

I want you to look at that little one and tell her everything that's about to come her way, everything that she doesn't yet know she's going to have to endure.

I remember when I was at my most heartbroken and hopeless, I came across a photo of myself as a child. And in the midst of completely breaking down, I realized that this little girl had no idea what she was going to have to go through in life. I looked at her and decided to tell her everything I knew. And oddly, even at my lowest point, it didn't end with me saying that the breakup I was going through was going to be The End for her.

You need to do the same. And then make your photo the screen saver and wallpaper on your phone.

Now I want you to imagine this: If you were walking down the street today and saw someone beating the living daylights out of that little girl, what would you do?

I am positive that you would intervene.

Guess what? You are *still* that same kid. That's *YOU.*

And not only are you beating her up, but you're letting everyone else have a go at her too. If you can't stick up for the adult that you are, you can most definitely stick up for the little one in that photo.

Soon you'll start to love and respect yourself for protecting her. And you will begin to attract people who value that little girl as much as you do because they, too, were able to find a way not out but *back* to that child who so desperately needed them.

If you continue to ignore her, you will never allow her to grow up. Every time you get triggered, you will regress to the emotional paralysis of the age that you were in that photo—on an endless search for unconditional, paternal love from toxic users.

I look at this kid who has no idea what's about to come her way, no idea how to be enough, and because of that, she spends every day trying to be everything that she doesn't know she already is.

I feel ashamed for the times I've ignored, abused, and minimized her. I hate myself for not protecting her, for allowing others to make her feel as defective and unworthy as I did. I hate that I clipped her wings by allowing her to be a victim for so long.

The key to unconditional confidence and self-love is not in the closure you think you need from shitty people. It's not in a book, a seminar, a blog, a workshop, or a trip around the world. There is no preparation required, and the conditions don't need to be perfect.

All it takes is getting out a photo of yourself as a child, looking at that voiceless, defenseless little soul, and making the decision right then and there to be the best friend, parent, big sister, confidante, and advocate that she did not have.

And only you know *exactly* what that kid wanted, needed, and did not have—not me, not your ex or your therapist or your friends and family—YOU.

Breakups have a way of activating old wounds and triggers and bringing up a bunch of bullshit and pain. Most people who are unable to advocate for themselves can easily do so for other people.

Forget about the adult that you are. Get out of the self-obsession for one minute. Focus on that little girl. Promise her that from this point forward, no one will ever fuck with her again and be the embodiment of everything she needed.

This is how I saved my own life and built the kind of confidence and self-love that no one can ever take away.

You can too.

Part 2

THE
WISDOM
OF A
WINNER

6

What Is He?

Y ou can't win anything if you don't know your "opponent" better than he knows himself. And if you are a true winner, which you are, you will get to know *yourself*—on a level that you never have before—in the process of studying the opposition.

As you continue to learn about what your ex is, there will be a strong desire but *never* a need to diagnose him to his face (or to anyone). Stay on your White Horse. This information is for *you* to weaponize against *your* fears (not your ex) so that you can win this breakup with dignity and indifference.

One of the first steps in getting over your ex is to understand exactly *what* you are dealing with.

Is he emotionally unavailable?

A narcissist? *A fuckboy?*

Whether it was a family member, a friend, or an ex, I know I've taken a lot of comfort in finding out exactly *what* I was dealing with. Not only was I able to better understand and accept that this person's behavior had nothing to do with me, but I was able to better understand and address my own issues as a result.

Being able to give an actual *name* to all the dysfunction that we think we are alone in experiencing is validating. It gives us an opportunity to replace the what-ifs and mixed signals with certainty that this type of person will never be capable of the relationship we want. It's nice to finally feel seen, understood, and heard after being with someone who could never see, understand, and hear anyone but himself.

So you go online and try to find the perfect article or video that can put a name to all this confusion. You want to find something that will nail every one of his traits, assure you that he will never change, and confirm you're not crazy.

I think it's very healthy and crucial to know what you're dealing with. The problem is, it's a slippery slope.

You may find that your ex fits the description of a narcissist perfectly, but when you look up the characteristics of one, he may not have *all* of them. There may be a lot of overlapping and conflicting information too. This creates an opportunity for false hope, doubt, self-blame, and obsession.

Researching every type of *what* he could be also gives you an excuse not to take any action in your own life. You investigate everything online that's similar to what you went through, but nothing ever gives you full surety of *exactly* what you are dealing with. Just when you think he's one thing, you'll learn about another new term and spin your wheels even more.

Sometimes it's easier to simplify and start (and, in some cases, end) with an irrefutable blanket term.

> **There is a common denominator of *every* type of person who cannot be in a mutual and mature relationship. Nor can they be consistent in valuing, respecting, and being honest with you.**
>
> **It's called toxicity.**

Some people are just shitty. Plain and simple. No matter how confident they appear or how many friends they have, these people hate themselves and are extremely insecure deep down. They are incapable of intimacy and only capable of shallow relationships (even though they like to represent themselves as having and craving depth). They drain you of your energy, are manipulative, emotionally unhealthy, and bring you down more than they *ever* bring you up.

Toxic people have a way of rationalizing betrayal and getting you to believe that you are the problem every time. This is why you always find yourself defending them to concerned family and fed-up friends.

These people use others to spew their own misery, issues, and bullshit. If they ever admit that they have a shortcoming, it's because they've realized they can fake self-awareness and vulnerability to reap the *benefits* of your love and empathy without having to back words up with action. Their sense of control comes from getting you to forfeit control over your own life, and they are a complete waste of time. They can only see themselves in the most exonerated, entitled, and righteous light.

Toxic people are empathetically bankrupt and selfish. Their hot-cold behavior generally comes from un-dealt with trauma in their childhood.

I have all the empathy in the world for anyone who was traumatized as a child (I don't think any of us exit childhood completely unscathed). Whether these people seek help and want to evolve is no one's business other than their own. But what I have no empathy for are grown adults who use their romantic relationships to revisit the scene of an emotional crime in their past, be a convenient victim when it serves them, and a manipulative puppet master when it does not. They do this as a way to invalidate the pain and *the people who caused that pain* in their childhood and past relationships.

Toxic people cannot make this connection, nor do they care to reflect on why they do what they do. The only thing they can genuinely connect to is their entitlement to everything of *yours* that they can only pretend to offer in return.

Here are some characteristics of toxic people:

* They think that different people deserve different versions of the truth. But no one ever gets the whole truth—including themselves. Delusion is at an all-time high.

* They are chameleons, always conforming to whatever person or group they're with. And no matter how much they like to think they're an alpha, they're just a minnow—forever trying to fit in and "lead the pack."

* They love pinning people against one another. The more people they can get to compete for their time, love, and attention, the better.

* They drop bombs of drama and then run away and innocently ask everyone if they know who or what started the explosion. They also love being the good

Samaritan, the "cleanup crew" for the bombs that, unbe-
knownst to others, *they* set off.

- They always have to be in control and get their way.

- They are the biggest hypocrites you will ever meet. And
  when you call them out on their hypocrisy, they will
  turn the tables. Within a matter of minutes, you will be
  apologizing to *them* for "overreacting" when really, you
  did nothing but make an accurate observation.

- They make you feel crazy and immature for wanting to
  rehash anything respectfully to gain clarity.

- The more they can get under your skin, the more they can
  make you jealous, insecure, and become the *only* source
  of your confidence and happiness (along with your insecurity and misery), the more important they feel.

- They have a doctorate in both signal mixing and
  mind fucking.

- They cannot be trusted.

- As much as they love seeing you unglue by making you
  feel jealous and envious, *they* are extremely jealous
  and envious of others.

- They lack authenticity. Their disingenuousness comes from an absence of healthy boundaries. And their "standards" are so superficial and impossible that you often wonder why they're even with you.

- They expect you to be loyal to them no matter what— even though they are traitorous, two-faced, and extremely disloyal.

- They treat YOU like the emotional infant that THEY are. Oftentimes, they will give you the silent treatment or psychologically school you on everything that they cannot embody, let alone practice.

- They are selfish. Everyone is a means to an end for these people. If it doesn't serve them, then it doesn't matter. Toxic people don't "see" other people. They will either see no opportunity to further their agenda and get their selfish needs met (someone who has healthy boundaries)—OR, they will see a possibility for a big return with zero investment (a doormat who is hungrier for a crumb of validation than retained dignity).

- They are incredible to their friends, family, and sometimes even exes from their past. But how "incredible" they are to you is contingent upon how much you excuse, provide, accommodate, and inflate their ego.

- They will allow and encourage you to own *their* shitty behavior. What they do is *always* because of something *you* did or did not do.

- Being in a relationship with them strains the relationships that you have with your family, friends, and most importantly, yourself.

- They always have to be right and WIN—every argument, discussion, and yes, *even their breakups.* These people always feel inferior, which means that they're always on the defense. This is why they can never be genuinely happy for other people; the success of others detracts from *their* sense of self. Hence, everything is a competition.

Toxic people are inconsistent. They love promising a future to get current needs met and red flags excused. They will pedestal you to heights you've never been before and then de-pedestal you to the point that you question your value as a human being and, sometimes, your need for being on this planet.

After a while of being on their roller coaster, you start to equate the intensity of that dangerous ride with "passion."

Passion is not about how often someone can change personalities, relational rules, moral codes, and the definition of honesty.

It's about consistently showing up because you love and value yourself enough to truly love and value someone else.

The cost of being in a relationship with a toxic person is always everything you can never afford to lose: your self-esteem, your standards, and your mental health (sometimes your finances as well). They may also isolate you from certain friends and family members of yours who they know can see right through them.

You may be thinking, "Natasha, you just defined a narcissist" or "a fuckboy" or "a gaslighter," but the *common denominator* is the same. That is the focus here—the *species*, as opposed to the various animals within that species.

I refer to these people as "toxic" because that is quite literally what they are—**poison**—to *your* peace, *your* mental health, and *your* well-being.

Do not get bogged down by the fact that other people like and hang out with them. Those people don't know them on the level that you do. And even if they do, they're not YOU.

Now that you have identified toxicity, you must make a committed decision to walk away from what is poisonous to *you*. **This comes from knowing who the fuck you are.** If you don't, you will spend the rest of your life around people who get off on feeding you emotional poison. And then they get to become the "hero" for holding your hair as you throw up and apologize for the mess.

After being diagnosed with celiac disease over ten years ago, I am committed to the decision I've made not to eat gluten. If I do, I'll experience physical symptoms that aren't just painful and unpleasant, but they affect the one thing that I am still, to this day, more conscious of than I wish I was: my appearance.

My face will break out in oozing eczema patches and pustules if I have gluten. I spent so many years with this mystery "acne" that no one could heal that I never want to have to experience that again. I didn't want to leave the house. My energy was depleted, and I felt terrible for years, not knowing that I was eating allergens every day.

I now know that gluten is toxic to *my* system. And as C.E.O. of *myself*, I made the executive decision to do what's best for my health and not eat it.

Do I cry every day about gluten "rejecting" me? No, I don't. My body rejected IT!

I don't wake up every morning, look in the mirror, and say to myself, "Natasha, you're going to try your hardest to avoid gluten today. If you see a baguette or a doughnut, run!" Nor do I call ahead of time to make sure the restaurant where my friends and I are eating at doesn't serve gluten because I know I'll cave and devour it if I see it.

I don't obsess over the millions of people in this world who can eat gluten and not experience the symptoms I do. And I don't go around town spreading "anti-gluten" propaganda, telling people that they shouldn't eat gluten. *What kind of life would that be?*

I rest easy knowing that the commitment to maintain my physical health is solid in a decision that has changed my life and turned the uncomfortable symptoms around.

The same goes for my mental health and toxic people.

A toxic person is anyone who gets validation by exploiting your hunger for theirs.

I have been an incredibly shitty person in my life. I used to lie pathologically, gossip compulsively, and was extremely bitter and jealous. I've cheated, and I've played games. I've not only taken good people for granted, but I've taken advantage of them and their genuine love for me. I don't say this in any kind of gratuitous way or in an attempt to create some grand juxtaposition and showcase how great I am now.

I am doing my imperfect best; we all are. I am still contradictory and a total hypocrite at times. I still feel jealous, insecure, and scared. I fail much more than I succeed. The only difference now is, I've found a way not to let all of those (very human) emotions and experiences permeate to the point of paralysis. THAT is what turned my life around—not morphing into some know-it-all who never has a bad day.

I think back to when I was toxic, and honestly, it never had anything to do with the other person. I never thought, "Hmm, I definitely don't think Joe is worth a call back. He's only worth a text!"

I would always do what was best for *me*.

I didn't act in terrible and selfish ways just so I could educate good people on their lack of worth. I acted in terrible and selfish ways because *I felt* worthless and was a toxic asshole.

I loved seeing other people get as unsure and insecure around me as I felt deep down. It gave me a sense of power in a life I had lost control of and felt powerless in. It was so sad and pathetic. I would do anything I could to avoid accountability and feel like I wasn't the only one. Even if that meant making good people second-guess themselves.

The same goes for your toxic ex.

You are reading this right now because your will to survive is greater than what has happened to you. Your ex can't say the same. His egoic survival is *dependent* on what he feels like he deserves—which is the affirmation that this breakup is breaking you down.

We all have an ego. Our ego is the part of us that survives only from *external* and *superficial* sources of validation.

I feel great when I post a photo of myself and get a bunch of comments and likes. I also love being appreciated, rewarded, and recognized for what I do. And I have to admit, when I get attention from people who fucked me over or when I hear that they are continuing to fail in life, it feels great.

That's the ego.

Thankfully, I am more indifferent to bullshit than I am interested in wasting time wishing ill on anyone who's treated me poorly. I'm more invested in making an impact for others than I am being the center of attention. And although I can admit that I like and appreciate outside validation, I don't *need* it to survive anymore.

I have dedicated my life to servitude. I live to help others get out of pain, confusion, self-hate, and suffering that I know all too well. I live to be everything my younger self needed and did not have. Nothing has healed my pain more than helping others out of theirs (starting with my younger self). Nothing has empowered me and transformed my life more than nongratuitously sharing my insecurities, fears, failures, heartbreak, and embarrassments so that others realize they were never alone in theirs.

This is how you give your pain a purpose. It's what allows you to accept that some people are lessons. Some relationships are mirrors, and not being ashamed of the reflection is what unblurs the line between toxic people (who were never worth one second of your time) and FAMILY (who understands, empathizes with, and supports you). It's what gets you over the heartbreak and able to celebrate the joy of being in the kind of self-awareness and gratitude that the toxic ones will never be able to experience.

> **Your ex will *never know* what it's like to get off the hamster wheel. He is on an endless search for bandages to put over the cancer of his inferiority complex.**

Toxic people are prisoners to shortcomings that they have no problem being in denial of. And they always end up proving through their actions that they are more interested in protecting their ego than being wrong (and evolving as a result of self-reflection, empathy, accountability, and communication).

> **In life, there are people who will use the dependency they trigger *you to have on them* as a way to feel better about themselves.**

And then there are people just like you who get hurt by these people. And although you are fallible (as we all are), look at you STILL searching for ways to better yourself while simultaneously blaming yourself for the behavior of a grown adult!

You don't have to do that anymore.

There are so many good people in this world who, just like you, can blossom, evolve, and thrive BECAUSE OF applying the lessons learned from heartbreak. People who are able to fully value and appreciate others because they value and appreciate everything they've done to fight for the unconditional self-love that no one can ever take away from them.

You are looking for employment but don't realize that you're already a C.E.O.

> **Your relationships do not define you. How you define yourself is what attracts the relationships you have. It's what sets the bar for everything you tolerate.**

I know this breakup made you feel worthless, but the way you were treated is not about you. It's a reflection of how this man feels about himself.

Every day, I try not to make anything about me. The less I make it about me, the more I heal and the more I can help others heal because my ego does not control me. If this book is a failure, it's because *I failed to deliver* the message that I want to deliver to *you*. It does not mean that I, Natasha Adamo, *am* a failure. I don't make it about me because it's not. This is about *you*.

The ego is as easily satisfied as it is desperate and fragile. And no matter how toxic your ex is, you felt valid just by being in a relationship with him. Now, that validation is gone, and your ego will do anything to secure its next supply. This is why you're so hungry for another crumb. Your ego literally needs that crumb to stay alive.

In the next chapter, I will get into how your ego became so amplified. But for now, know this: When the ego starts to starve, it will haunt you until you either submit or checkmate it through internal validation. If you're operating from the place of your ego, whatever you see your ex do (or notice that he doesn't do) on social media will send you into a tailspin. This is because you are literally depending on someone else to dictate your worth and emotional weather.

> **You are chasing the high of external validation more than you are chasing the substance of a worthwhile man.**

Toxic people are driven *exclusively* by their egos. At least you have enough awareness to give your pain a purpose and make a clean break out of this. Your ex will always be a prisoner to his ego.

He needs the reassurance that you don't know who the fuck you are or where your White Horse went.

He needs to know that you'll always be there to inflate him back up when he feels exposed, caught, and undesirable.

When toxic people take a hit to the ego (and get introduced to your boundaries, standards, and silence), they will start making obnoxious promises that go beyond what they can deliver.

They'll tell you that they've changed, that they're sorry and miss you. They'll get sentimental and nostalgic.

They also may not say anything at all.

You'll suddenly see on social media that they made a big life change or started dating someone new. They may even go completely silent but still follow you and like the photos you post. This is all just another way that they can passively yank your chain, curate their of-the-moment image, and fish for reactions.

Toxic people get so overcome by their own insecurities, fear, and lack of control that they'll do anything to secure a feeling of superiority. This is why your ex will ghost you or won't reply for hours on end when you finally respond to him.

You've already given him enough of what he needed.

Even if you write back and tell him to leave you alone, it will be enough to feed his ego (and enough for yours to starve to the point of wanting more from a man who does not have more to give). He'll know that he got under your skin and that at the very least, you still give enough shits to reply.

It is not hard to jump-start your ex's ego, but it is *impossible* to jump-start a closed heart, a disconnected conscience, and emotional intelligence that just isn't there.

The ego is inconsistent. It's like a frantic junkie who doesn't care about where the drug came from or how sterile the needle is. It just needs a hit. And because your ex's ego is never satisfied (as all egos are), there is no way to ensure that *you* will always be the scratch that relieves that itch. *Do you really want to live the rest of your life never truly knowing where you stand with your partner?* Are you going to continue fetishizing a painful land of limbo? Or do you want to get away from the poison and become irreplaceable?

Loving yourself enough not to need any outside validation and walking away from what you know is poisonous to *you*—THAT is what makes you an irreplaceable C.E.O. You are no longer anyone's employee.

When you learn to validate yourself:

- **You'll be able to see your ex for *what* he really is—** an emotional infant throwing a fit because he hates not being able to sit at the adult's table. He hates being trapped in the playpen of his ego, which is why he has to make his life seem so exclusive and exciting.

- **You'll start to be attracted to what's good for you instead of what triggers you into trying to be "good enough."**

- **You'll stop feeling obligated to people whom you didn't even like to begin with.**

- **Chain yanks will no longer faze you. You'll be able to tell the difference between a strong, empathetic man who actually *wants* you and a fragile ego that *needs* your reactivity to live to see another day.**

- **You'll let go of the people in your life who are holding you back and not allowing you to evolve.** Anyone who depletes you is out; anyone who enriches your life is in.

- **You'll appreciate good men (yes, they are out there) instead of taking them for granted, writing them off, and going back to pining over the potential of emotional bums.**

- **You'll be able to connect with other people from a place of genuine interest.** No more insecurity, fear, and feeling cool just because you're associated with someone you've pedestaled.

Keep this in mind when it comes to your toxic ex:

IT'S NOT HIM THAT YOU CAN'T GET OVER— IT'S WHAT HE *REPRESENTED*.

The only time your ex didn't try to dim your light is when it was shining on him. YOU shined YOUR light on him and then became awestruck by the glowing, "self-illuminated" man. You thought that he was your light; your sole source of warmth, shelter, and happiness when really, it was YOU, the entire time—shining *your* light on him.

Your ex was not the "greatest man you've ever known." *You* were the greatest you had ever been when you were with him.

You have struggled with boundaries and self-love your entire life, which is why you fall for men who make you love the person you are when you're around them. You were able to do things for your ex that you couldn't do for yourself (like protect, nurture, encourage, and support). **He is not the greatest.** The *idea* that you had of him and what he *represented* was the greatest. And all that credit you're giving him—he didn't earn it. Give *yourself* some credit for finally putting the poison down.

Do you remember how you continued to love, encourage, and believe in him despite all the red flags, lies, and mixed signals? It's time to believe in *yourself* that way despite all the heartbreak, fear, and self-doubt.

IF HE JUST WANTS SEX, THAT DOES NOT MAKE HIM TOXIC.

There are plenty of men who respectfully communicate up front about just wanting to get laid with no strings attached—and there's nothing wrong with that! What makes someone toxic is the *misrepresentation*. It's saying one thing and having the selfish *agenda* to do another.

YOUR EX MAY KNOW HE'S TOXIC, OR HE MAY HAVE NO CLUE.

It doesn't matter and it's not your job to be an educational resource center for anyone but yourself. Shitty, disrespectful behavior will always be shitty, disrespectful behavior. There is no such thing as a "part-time" toxic person. Just like there's no such thing as "half-gluten" pizza that I can eat.

IT DOESN'T MATTER HOW NICE HE IS TO OTHER PEOPLE.

It doesn't matter how philanthropic he is or how many times he brings his grandmother groceries. It doesn't matter if he's literally reinventing the wheel or curing cancer as you read this. What matters is that he consistently treated YOU in a less than manner. And that will always be enough to confirm his toxicity. Great, connected, and empathetic people don't just conveniently run out of character, communication skills, and integrity.

IT DOESN'T MATTER HOW MUCH YOU MISS HIM AND HOW GOOD HIS INTENTIONS WERE.

Let's get real about what you actually miss here. Remember, you are missing all of the hopes and dreams that he *represented* the actualization of—not who he *really* is.

Think of the litany of deplorable behavior you were on the receiving end of. Think of your incredible friends and family who love you. Think of your unborn child looking down on you right now, cheering you on to flush the shit and meet someone who can meet you halfway (so that you can meet your baby sooner). Think of your own child/children (if you already have them) or your nieces and nephews who are counting on you to lead by example over words. Think of your younger self who relies on you to be her advocate.

You've spent hours telling everyone how terribly he treated you. Yet you're convinced that he's got a big heart, is a lonely victim, and "means well." *Who cares if someone has a "big heart" or they "mean well" if they don't behave as such?* And if someone is wounded (and they're not a wild animal or an unruly toddler), they shouldn't automatically default to wounding others.

He doesn't mean well—he only means to get HIS NEEDS met.

One of the biggest challenges I faced when trying to move on from a toxic ex was the belief that his intentions weren't bad. I was so desperate to get him back; I had no choice but to dumb myself down by holding on to his "good intentions." As long as he was well intended, I was the problem (and could continue to stay invested). This was the only way I could avoid the shame of having to accept the truth—that people are what they consistently *do*—not who they represent themselves to be in the first five minutes of knowing them.

THIS IS NOT ABOUT VILIFYING YOUR EX AND CLAIMING THAT HE'S SOME KIND OF MONSTER.

Not all toxic people are bad people. Some of them really do care for and love us. The problem is, their definition of care and love is much different than ours. This causes us to constantly negotiate down (and ultimately sacrifice) our identity, boundaries, standards, and values *just to be in ANY kind of relationship with them.* And THAT is toxic. It's poisonous to *our* mental health.

Remember, everything that you are feeling and experiencing right now is a direct result of your tolerations. In life, you will always get what you consistently CHOOSE to put up with. Now that you know *what* your ex is, you need to decide *what exactly* you are no longer willing to tolerate.

Killing your list in Chapter 1 allowed you to rise from your ashes, but staying on your White Horse is what *keeps you* above them. It's what creates that Je Ne Sais Quoi, X-Factor that everyone is attracted to, wants to know more about, and wants a piece of but can't quite describe or put their finger on.

Do you know how rare it is to come across someone who doesn't feel like they have to advertise who they are, collect validation tokens, and prove their worth?

You will never again be preoccupied with whether anyone likes you, approves of you, agrees with you, or misses you because you love you—infinitely and unconditionally.

Your ex is expecting you to play games right now. If you do, he'll get affirmation that you're just as insecure as you've always been and he'll know that he won this breakup. But when you behave like a winner who doesn't have time for dumb games because you realize that you actually won by *losing* him and all of his drama…

That's when he will truly feel the loss of you and all that you are.

If you are indifferent, confident, detached, and happy, he will stalk the shit out of you and obsess to no end. He will stop at nothing to find out what got into you and whom you're with because his ego has taken a major hit. You may never be aware of this, but just because he's not directly reaching out, that doesn't mean he's not acting on his curiosity behind closed doors. **You were treated terribly and look at how invested you *still* are.** You were invested enough to pick up this book! Don't think for one second that your ex won't act on the curiosity that your dignity and silence ignite in him.

Remember *what* your ex is. He is toxic, and toxic people are only capable of selfish regret, not genuine remorse. He will only feel the loss of you in a selfish way. He will miss the you that kept providing for him, while turning a blind eye to all of his disrespectful behavior.

Toxic people are incapable of operating outside of themselves and their needs because they are trapped in their ego.

> **And you deserve so much more than a triggered ego and a few crumbs.**

> **You deserve an open *HEART*.**

Don't rely on words to travel fast. Words get minced and talk is cheap. Energy travels even faster than words. Communicate through your actions what you are no longer willing to put up with, and believe me, the energetic antennas of toxic people, near and far, will go up immediately upon release of your newly defined signal.

> **The moment you tell yourself "he fell out of love with me" is the moment you acknowledge that he's capable of love. The moment you tell yourself "he fell out of need" . . .**

> **That is the moment you acknowledge the user he *is*, the doormat you *were*, and the poison you will no longer ingest.**

I love the term "toxic" because unlike "fuckboy" there's no hateful, bitter, or triggered charge to it.

He's just toxic. And you're just *THAT* detoxed.

7

Understanding What Got You Here

This Is Why Toxic Relationships Are So Addictive

Y ou've detoxed by gaining an understanding of your ex's toxicity (an understanding that he doesn't even have) and using that awareness to address your own. But in order to prevent retox, you need to be able to get to the root of your *addiction* to toxic relationships. If you don't, the cycle will continue, your loneliness will make setting boundaries impossible, and your ex will get confirmation that you are more desperate than dignified.

The hardest thing I've ever had to do is get clean from my addiction to toxic relationships and toxic people.

Now, when I read that sentence, it's like saying, "The hardest thing I've ever had to do is flush a toilet." But when you've spent your whole life people-pleasing, it's difficult to realize that with members of the toxic species, it's actually impossible to lose them.

They lose YOU.

But it didn't feel that way.

I had lost the three most important relationships in my life:

1. **An ex whom I was still convinced was my soulmate** (even though he was selfish, had a limited relationship with reality, and made me feel like I was hard to love).

2. **Friends whom I thought would be around forever** (even though they proved to be fake).

3. **Family members who were supposed to be there always** (even though they were never all "there" to begin with). They got off on dangling the carrot of their approval my entire life.

No one was trying to get back in my life and it really hurt. It felt like everyone I had never given up on, decided to give up on me, once *I decided* to have limits.

The books I read reinforced my decision to get clean, but nothing addressed why I was still so desperate for what I knew was unhealthy. I wanted to know what programmed me; what got me to this place of only seeing the good in people I had to be "good enough" for.

Why was I only attracted to relationships that I had to provide, prove myself, and fight for?

A lot of the information I found focused on positive thinking, which is great until you start feeling like a failure for not being able to shift to positivity at any given time. Yes, having a positive mindset is the foundation of living a healthy and happy life. But I couldn't just positively think my way out of a relapse I was itching to engage in and away from an addiction I've had since as early as I can remember (and did not understand).

I know how badly you want to get clean. I also know how much your heart misses what your intuition *knows* is poisonous to your system.

I know how much of a punishment the loneliness feels like right now. Especially when you've always shown up for a man who isn't showing up for you. A man who hurt you *after* you let down your guard and took the time to explain your pain to him.

The only way to get through the withdrawals and get clean is to understand that you did not choose this addiction. You were set up, long ago, by well-intended people who were doing the best they could—all while trying to avoid *their own* withdrawals and deny the shame of *their own* addiction to approval.

Remember, we all have an ego.

Winning this breakup and being able to call your own relational shots from here on out is dependent on one thing and one thing only. It's dependent on whether you want to live the rest of your life on your knees; performing for the approval crumbs of others because your ego dominates you, or *you* want to dominate *it*—as C.E.O. of YOU.

As we discussed in the last chapter, our ego is the part of us that depends on external sources of validation for survival. To understand your ego better, we have to once again go back to the beginning. Here's how your ego turned you into a doormat.

As a child, you were taught that nothing worth having comes easy.

At some point, conditional love was given to you by a parent or parental figure whom you unconditionally loved and relied on for emotional safety. And because you only received crumbs of a loaf that was your birthright, this robbed you of the opportunity to learn how to make your own loaves and emotionally feed yourself.

You did NOT (and do not) have to beg, perform, or settle for crumbs ever. *But what other option did you have back then?* The adults whom you depended on to lead by example had not yet figured this out for themselves.

As you grew up, you came to the table starving in every relationship you formed. This is because you were starved at your most impressionable stage by adults who, although loved you and gave you everything they could, were subconsciously trying to satiate their own hunger and did not know how.

With no tools to turn inward, seeking *external* validation became your only option.

You were always putting on a show, trying to give and be "enough" for family, friends, and teachers. **This normalized perfectionism AND toxic relationships for you.** As you grew up, you became attracted to what triggered you into "audition mode" (toxic people) instead of what nourished your mental health (people who didn't need to use *your need* for their approval to feel significant).

I used to be convinced that the key to my happiness and value could be found in everything outside of the person I'd never be (until, of course, I could afford certain material items and become "good/pretty/popular/cool enough" to land a certain type of friend group and man). I relied on the superficial because I was never taught how to amplify the substantial, which took over two decades to realize

I was born with. This gave way to self-sabotage, people-pleasing, and an attraction to men whose character negated how great they looked on paper.

Toxic people need reassurance that you are hungry for their validation. It's the only way they can get the validation that they are just as hungry for. And because we will never put up with anyone treating us any worse than we are *already* treating ourselves in one way or another...

An addiction to toxic relationships requires that you have a toxic relationship *with* yourself.

Whenever you get a crumb of validation from your ex, you work that much harder to get more. After getting a few crumbs, you mush them together and proudly show off your "loaf." But it never feels as good as you know it should because it's not a real loaf. It's just a bunch of crumbs that you had to mush together. So you work even harder to get that loaf because your thinking goes, if he didn't have a loaf hidden somewhere, there would be no crumbs to throw your way.

Crumbs then become an indication of something more instead of what they really are—a sign that you *deserve* more.

This is why potential turns you on more than good guys who are "too nice" and "boring." They're boring because you don't have to put on a dog and pony show to get an obligatory crumb thrown your way.

They're "too nice" because they don't support or exploit your warped relational belief system that "nothing worth having comes easy."

Becoming attracted to quality men was never about learning how to "settle" or hypnotizing myself into being turned on by trolls. I was attracted to men who were toxic because I had no self-respect; I lacked boundaries. And as long as you don't have respect for yourself, you'll never have respect for anyone who genuinely respects you—no matter how much you claim to want and deserve it.

> **As much as you want a man to see in you everything that you cannot see in yourself, if you don't have to "work hard" for him to go from completely blind to 20/20 vision, all attraction is lost.**

And even though it's great to live your life with the mantra "It's the little things that matter," if it's crumbs that matter the most to you, that's not living an admirable life. That's living in a state of delusion, starvation, and addiction that has gotten so out of hand that you need to get clean. Right now.

Here's why toxic relationships are so addictive.

THEY HAVE THE BEST MOMENTS.

Toxic people have a way of giving us the greatest, most never-be-fore-experienced highs that somehow make the lows—as deal breaking as they are—impossible to walk away from.

The worst relationships have the best moments.

But that's all they are—MOMENTS. And you deserve so much more than a lifetime of having to string moments and mush crumbs together.

The moments feel so incredible and irreplaceable not because they really are, but because low self-esteem (and the hunger and desperation it breeds) will make you focus more on the high of satiation than the shame of starvation. When you're THAT hungry, **anything** will make you feel amazing and bring you back to life. A piece of moldy bread will have you feeling so good that you'll be convinced that it's from a five-star restaurant.

Instead of addressing your level of starvation, which is so bad, it has you believing that mold is a delicacy. You focus on the satiation —how *incredible* it makes you feel. This sets you up to overvalue the crumbs and pedestal the man throwing them your way. You're convinced that he's some kind of prodigy with a "magic touch" when really, it was just your level of hunger that allowed A CRUMB to satiate you.

VALUE INCREASES IF THE SUPPLY IS LIMITED.

It's human nature to place more value on something if the supply is limited. We want it even more when we know that not everyone can get it.

And although that's great if you're referring to an exotic car or a pair of shoes, if things like honesty, integrity, communication, respect, maturity, and empathy are in limited supply, that does not make them, or the man not possessing 100 percent of them, more valuable. It makes you more addicted to affirming your perceived *lack* of value than you are acting on your *inherent* value—by getting on your White Horse and riding away from the bullshit.

HIGH HIGHS AND LOW LOWS.

Toxic relationships are not slow, steady, and consistent. They are a roller-coaster ride of yes/no, hot/cold, up/down, Jekyll/Hyde that usually mirror your childhood/un-dealt with trauma in some way.

And just because there is an inconsistent thread of something more, something deeper, something *approaching* intimacy, that doesn't make the relationship any more romantic or any less hurtful. It just makes it more *addictive*—by pumping your poor nervous system with adrenaline for a roller coaster that it isn't built to ride.

I believe that this is a big reason why emotional dis-ease is now being linked more than ever to physical diseases.

After a while, you become addicted to the *intensity* of that ride and mistake it for a passionate, soulmate connection. When it's no longer there, you go into withdrawal. The withdrawal is so unbearable that you go back every time, dumbing yourself down with things like, "Oh, but the sex is so good" and "We fight as hard as we love!"

But how good can the sex *really* be if you have to essentially turn a blind eye to the *person* that a body part is attached to?

AUDITIONING.

What woman wouldn't want to feel like she was so special she got to be The Chosen One over all the other options a man had? That she was so exceptional, she got to *be* the exception to a rule that not even his closest friends and family ever thought that *anyone* would be the exception to? This is what the most memorable fairy tales and love stories (in books and on-screen) are made of.

The problem with auditioning is that it inspires *acting*, not connecting. And this is not a television show. This is your life that you get only one of.

Toxic relationships are addictive because of your wiring. You were primed to perform. And just like in your childhood, you still feel like you have to "audition" to get the role of a lifetime. Whatever you have to do, you'll do it. Like a true method actor, you'll change, contort, and morph into anything you have to become—just to be chosen for a part to play. This reminds me of when I was applying to universities. I put so much effort into being the perfect student for the university that I didn't take any time to see if the university was even right for me.

Stop telling yourself things like, "What if he doesn't miss me?" "What if he doesn't choose me?"

What if YOU don't miss or choose *him*?

TRIANGLES.

With toxic relationships, you're always in a triangle of some kind, trying to outbid the highest bidder. There's a constant need to "beat the competition" and be chosen over someone or something that's getting your partner's attention. This could be an ex, his family, friends, job, hobbies, the porn accounts he follows, every other woman he notices when you're out in public, anything.

The point is, it's never just you and him.

It's you, him, and this other person or entity that he knows makes you feel threatened. You feel like you have to work that much harder to get the attention and loyalty that he withholds from you but gives freely to the other point in the triangle.

Newsflash: True love is not triangular—it's linear. **In one of the most famous love songs of all time, Johnny Cash sings about** *walking the LINE* **for his partner**—not the triangle, octagon, or quadratic equation.

TUG OF WAR.

Nothing is ever equal, mutual, or on a level playing field in a toxic relationship. It's two relational gladiators competing for control over the other person.

When one hurts the other, they'll promise to do better and then trigger and relentlessly punish them while pretending to do so. It's a never-ending drama. The need to prove and disprove takes precedence over connecting because a genuine connection is impossible here.

Toxic relationships are a war of two *egos*, not a connection of two hearts.

Somewhere along the way, we bought into a very ignorant belief that the ultimate relationship goal is getting a man to "eat out of the palm of your hand," be "on a tight leash," and go into some sort of hypnotic trance just because you're tactically ambiguous.

Fortunately, you have become hungrier for more than these stupid games. Life is tough enough. Who wants to have to engage in some sort of formulaic warfare or feel like you need to emotionally, sexually, and communicatively withhold just to keep someone "on their toes" and interested?

That's not love; that's insanity.

You should never take advantage of someone's triggers just so you can feel better about yourself. Withholding your own abundance will never attract emotional abundance in the opposite sex.

You don't need to be reduced to psychological infancy and follow a certain "rule" or adopt some new, anxiety-inducing technique. This is old, outdated, and fundamentally a never-ending tug-of-war that's dependent on push-pull for survival.

Whether it's done consciously or subconsciously, toxic relationships *have to* be about controlling, triggering, and tearing the other person down. This is because each individual has failed to achieve the emotional maturity, discipline, and *self*-control that can only come from totally controlling the position as C.E.O. of YOU.

Both people are looking to emotionally "employ" the other (with the most impossible standards), but they can't even be "in business" for themselves! Neither individual can unconditionally love themselves enough to set boundaries and become an *emotional* entrepreneur, which is why these relationships always end with what feels like an unbearable amount of unfinished business.

The reason why this dynamic becomes so addictive is that you always feel like you have to have "the final say," like you can't leave unless you "get the power back." You tell yourself and your exhausted family and friends that "this is the last time."

It never is.

Gaining satisfaction from being able to hold the puppet strings over a situation or person is not true love. Nor is trying to change someone into what your ego needs them to be.

Love is not about how much you can tolerate or how much confidence you can lose in the process of building up your partner's.

It's about loving yourself enough to *act* on "enough!"

Only then will you be able to attract the relationship you've wanted because you've finally established it with yourself.

8

Understanding What *Kept* You Here

This Is Why Toxic Partners Are So Addictive

Killing your ex with kindness drains you of your power and self-respect. Torching him with indifference amplifies the light he dimmed and reinstates the one thing that he is scared shitless of you realizing: your worth.

You now know what got you here, but what's actually keeping you in this chokehold?

Why are you still addicted to your toxic ex?

He didn't value you in your relationship with him because he was too busy prioritizing deal breakers like:

- His need to impress his coworkers, friends, family, and every member of the opposite sex over you.

- Being an epic "moment curator," creating the most incredible MOMENTS and then surrounding those moments with consistent lies, manipulation, and mixed signals.

- Showering you with attention, intensity, and then going ice cold. This activated your mommy and/or daddy issues, set off your fear of abandonment, and ultimately allowed you to be desperate enough to morph into his selfish-need concierge.

- Following trashy accounts on social media and liking disrespectful photos for everyone to see.

- Attention-mongering at every turn.

- Manipulating situations to propel his selfish agenda.

- Always wanting to be in control and then becoming a convenient victim only when it served him.

- Triangulating to make you feel jealous and then
  the moment you have a human reaction, crazy-
  labeling you.

And the list goes on. So why is someone like this *still* so attractive to you?

Here's why toxic partners are so addictive—even after you realize that they are toxic.

THEIR BEST IS BELIEVABLE, AND THEIR WORST IS YOUR FAULT.

They have a way of making you believe that when they're at their best, THAT'S who they really are. And when they're at their worst, well, that's a consequence of who *you* are; it's your fault.

This sets you up to "investigate," all while you spin your wheels, stick around longer than you need to, try harder, and get used. You'd rather stay in the relationship and continue to be disrespected than know you were nothing more than a professional launching pad. You can't risk losing him and having him be "who he really is" with a woman who's everything you're not.

When our fears of rejection and abandonment are activated, it's difficult for us to realize that toxic people are *incapable* of reciprocating honesty, loyalty, and love. This makes a mutual and healthy relationship *impossible*.

Your ex had to appear honest, loyal, and loving in the beginning, but it was all an act. It was the only way he could secure a continuous supply of all the *value* (everything you provided and did for him) that you didn't have boundaries in place to protect.

THEY LOOK GREAT ON PAPER.

And because we are so reliant on the superficial, it's always about impressing other people instead of our younger self (who's all alone, doesn't give a shit about wealth or six-pack abs, and relies on *our judge of character* to survive). We'd rather have a good-looking holiday card to send out and an enviable social media feed instead of a real life that's bullshit- and drama-free.

The only people who are going to be impressed with how good looking of a couple you are, how many degrees he has, or how many balls he can throw at a professional level are the ones who are just as superficially based (and just as unattractive on the inside).

You still have a chance to get clean. There's a whole world of incredible people out there who are beautiful in ways that time can never mess with. And you're one of them, so start acting like it.

THEY ARE FAMILIAR.

They remind you of the parent or parental figure whom you could never be perfect enough for, the one who put conditions around love that you unconditionally gave to them. They also may remind you of an ex or a toxic person in your past. (This can be conscious or subconscious.)

I have done this so many times that I could put a picture of my parents in this book right now and write, "This is a photo of 99 percent of the men I've dated." **My advice to you is this:** If the man you're with very specifically reminds you of a parent, an ex, or someone who broke you in the past, RUN.

If you would not have physical sex with one of your parents, stop engaging in emotional incest with partners who remind you of them. **You will never get them to consistently give you everything that your parents withheld.** Getting someone to change will not invalidate the pain that a parent, an ex, or a bully from your past caused. Parenting and protecting your younger self will take care of that.

THEY'RE A LOT OF FUN BUT ONLY ON A SURFACE LEVEL.

Toxic partners are some of the most fun people to hang out with, but that's where it ends—on a superficial level.

If you're unfortunate enough to be in a romantic relationship with one, you'll always feel like you are the problem. You'll see how much their friends and family love them, and suddenly, you'll feel like you're too uptight and unreasonable for expecting basic relational necessities.

THEIR MISTAKES ARE YOUR FAULT.

They make you feel like you "made them" do it, like you put too much pressure on them.

I will expand on this in the next section, but bottom line, no one can make anyone do anything. Your behavior could have been the proverbial lubricant for your ex to behave a certain way, but ultimately, the capacity to carry out the actions that he chose to are his and his alone.

The only thing you can do is allow and enable capacities that were *preexisting*.

THEY MAKE YOU FEEL CERTAIN THAT THEY'VE CHANGED.

Toxic people send you down a path of addictively wondering about whether they have changed. When you're in a relationship with a toxic partner, he'll tell you (this is an exaggerated example) that he's allergic to your dog, will never get married, is a vegetarian, and afraid of heights. Then a few months after he breaks up with you, he'll post a photo proposing to his new fiancée on a plane, about to skydive, eating a steak, and holding a dog.

This would make women with even the highest levels of confidence and self-love question why they were a better preparer (for another woman) than they were a partner (to an "irreplaceable gentleman").

You wonder why weren't you "good enough" to be The One that got him to change his ways. She must be everything you're not. HOW ELSE could she be getting such a return on everything YOU invested? All the love that you wanted him to reciprocate is being given to someone who just came into the picture, and now, you're left in the dust.

What you're forgetting here is not everything that glitters is gold. This man has *already proven* to be fool's gold.

Instead of questioning your worth and getting upset that he "changed" for another woman, why not get weirded out that someone could completely switch lifestyles, personalities, and moral codes in the blink of an eye? And *all* because YOU are no longer in their life? Wow.

You have more than enough evidence to be skeptical. Yet, instead, you're convinced that the evidence you have is inadmissible. Making it about your lack of value is so much more convenient than doing the one thing you couldn't do as a defenseless child: *let grown adults own their own behavior.*

> **If your ex was selfish, disrespectful, and toxic enough to do what he did and say what he said to you, he's never going to be empathetic enough to see anything from anyone's perspective other than his own.**

> **He's also not going to meet someone, take absolutely no time to evolve, and then just transform into everything he could never consistently be with you.**

Toxic people love to show off. Just because he's supposedly giving this new woman everything that he never gave to you, this doesn't mean he's not giving it to other women on the internet and in real life too. You never know what happens behind unlocked cell phones and closed doors. Do not vilify her or attempt to educate her on what you know. She is a nonentity in your life and doesn't yet know what you already do.

Be kind to other women and mind your own business. He isn't with a woman who's better in every way. He's with a woman who is more tolerant of his bullshit because she's still blind to everything that you are no longer blind to. There is nothing to envy or worry about.

> **Your ex did not change. He revealed himself over *time* as he got more comfortable (and more certain of what you'd forgive and excuse).**

This isn't to say that toxic people are not capable of change. I am living proof that they are capable of it. But that change wasn't as simple as meeting a great guy after treating my ex terribly, taking no time to self-reflect, and being fresh out of a relationship. It took unplugging from patterns that produced such debilitating fear, doubt, and loneliness that I didn't think I would make it through the withdrawals. It took an uncomfortable look at what I had become, acknowledging my hypocrisy, and *owning* my own behavior for the first time. It took making the decision to stop being a victim and prioritize my younger self so I could get off my emotional ass and serve *her* instead of my ego.

Real and lasting change doesn't "just happen" because you meet someone new. It will only start to happen when you are ready to replace avoidance with honesty and rose-colored glasses with an intuition that is *acted* on and no longer ignored.

Your ex doesn't think that there's anything wrong with the way he is and operates. This is not the time to contact him and explain why his behavior is wrong. This is the time for you to own where you *went wrong* and adjust accordingly.

Remembering who the fuck you are and realizing your worth amid a painful breakup is scary and lonely. It takes TIME. It will break you in ways that you are convinced you have already broken and cannot break anymore. But if you allow the unconditional love that you have for your younger self to unbreak your heart, finish your ex's fragmented explanations, and answer your own questions, you will bounce back an unfuckwithable winner every time. A winner who is on her White Horse—with healthy boundaries and raised standards guiding the way.

When you make the commitment to change your ways and become the person you needed and never had (instead of the person that your ex wants, for now), that's when you'll stop worrying about him changing.

The kind of change you're worried about takes so much more than a social media post, a new job, a haircut, a trip around the world, a new partner, or even getting engaged. **It takes the courage to look yourself in the eye every day when you've spent your entire**

life avoiding the mirror. Real change requires that you make compassionate contact with the parts of yourself that have for so long been misunderstood. The parts of you that are insecure, scared, avoidant, and frozen in shame. It takes realizing that these attributes are not a definition of who you are but rather the only way you could emotionally cope, make sense of, and "contain" the pain of your past.

Genuine change takes an unwavering refusal to be a helpless victim, the empathy to know where you have betrayed others, and the awareness that these betrayals took place because, just like the adults in your childhood, you turned your back on your younger self. It takes the kind of commitment that your ex has already proven to be incapable of *as a friend* to you, let alone a partner in a romantic relationship.

If it were that easy to change, you wouldn't still be reading this book! You would have already realized that the real "win" was *losing* him, and you'd move on. So why are you giving your ex more credit here, expecting that he can genuinely change in the blink of an eye and you can't change *at all*?

Maybe one day, he will change. Maybe one day, it'll snow on the beach in Maui. But by that time, it won't matter to you anymore. You'll be indifferent because you changed long ago. And you didn't waste your life waiting around in a ski mask on the beach. You went where there was snow.

Right now, your ex is only capable of switching up a *facade*.

You have single-handedly torn down your own facade. You have risen above your own ashes and are now rebuilding—on a foundation that's more solid than he will *ever* have the opportunity to stand on.

Looking back, I can see exactly what I was doing to *attract* toxic relationships.

I WAS BEING POLITE AT THE EXPENSE OF MY BOUNDARIES, WHICH TURNED ME INTO A DOORMAT.

It's important to be polite, but when it comes to toxic people, being polite to them will always mean that you can't be polite to your younger self. I would always try to "play it cool." I'd say, "Oh, no worries. It's okay" if I had been stood up, ignored, or flat-out humiliated. I didn't have confidence or self-love, which made me that much more inclined to play the part of the "cool girl," who was laid-back, easygoing, and understanding to the point of being nothing more than an option to use when needed. I didn't want to make it seem like I was being needy or putting pressure on the relationship. This made it easy for toxic people to get *their* needs met while I continued to excuse disrespect and overvalued fleeting moments of decency.

I WAS A PROJECT MANAGER/MOMMY.

I would outsource all the unconditional paternal love that I wished would boomerang back to me. And when you're the mommy in a romantic relationship, a toxic partner will take advantage of that unconditional paternal love, but sexually, he will be attracted to women who do not parent or micromanage him. No one wants to have sex with a parent, and you shouldn't be parenting anyone but your younger self. A healthy relationship involves *two people* who actively parent their younger selves, not each other.

I also loved being a fixer. Projects and potential were so much more exciting than having to acknowledge the disaster of a person I was being exposed to in real time. I would find myself "if-ing" everything. "If he just dealt with his trust issues, everything would be perfect." "If he just felt comfortable enough, to be honest, we could take our relationship to the next level." I listened to words when I should have been listening to actions and patterns.

I OUTSOURCED UNCONDITIONAL LOVE AND EMPATHY.

Toxic people are empathetically bankrupt, but they're incredible at absorbing all the empathy you have for them so that you're left with none for yourself. I would listen to their endless stories of getting hurt and screwed over, and I would feel so sorry for them. I would then be the advocate for them that I couldn't be for my younger self. Of course, they only cared about being heard, so they never asked me about my past or my feelings unless they had to get a selfish need met.

I HAD A TYPE.

When describing the type of man I used to be attracted to, I never said "trustworthy," "honest," "consistent," "communicative," "loyal," "shared values," "wanting a committed relationship," "emotionally intelligent," or "empathetic." Instead, he had to be six feet tall, athletic, funny, charming, gainfully employed, good in bed (I didn't even know what that truly meant at the time), and the life of the party.

Now when I think about that list, it makes me feel nauseous and ashamed. I felt so low about myself that I figured that if I could date one of the "cool kids," I would finally get to be one by default.

The problem was when I would meet a man who had the super-ficial qualities I was looking for, there was always an absence of *substantial* ones. This is because I never put any emphasis on that to begin with. The lack of self-awareness, empathy, honesty, and character made a mutual relationship impossible. And instead of learning my lesson and focusing more on what matters most (and what I personally needed to work on within myself), I made sure that the next guy had a different look, job, hobbies, and lifestyle from the most recent one who broke my heart. This never worked because I was, again, going for a different animal but the same (toxic) *species*.

If you want to be in a relationship with a man who uses you until he has an opportunity to stand on greener grass, affirms your inse-curities and negative belief system via triangulation, and makes you feel more alone in his presence than if you were physically alone BUT looks incredible on paper, your "type" is toxic.

If you want to get clean, attract a man whose *shadow* will be brighter than your ex at his most amplified, and live the life of an emotional entrepreneur, understand this:

> **The moment you give substantial meaning to your ex's superficial qualities, that is the moment you give him the power to rob you of an identity, an appetite for more, and a life.**

Your ex's life will never be his own. He's too busy manufacturing crumbs, moments, and facades. He will forever be an employee of his ego.

Your life as C.E.O. just started. And it's addiction-free.

9

You're Not That Desperate

It's normal to feel like you'll never win this breakup, get over this heartbreak, and become indifferent to your ex, but you will. How fast that happens depends on whether you **truly believe** you're worth more than what you've tolerated—and you act according to that belief.

The results you get in life are a direct product of what you choose to tolerate.

You will never "settle" your way into:

* Being The One That Got Away

* A mutual, loving relationship

- The life you want

- Staying on your White Horse

- Knowing your worth

- Winning this breakup

Settling happens when desperation (and the emotional exhaustion it causes) overrides your intuition. And you are the furthest thing from desperate. You are here with me, right now, because you want to drop the mic on your ex and his toxicity.

Winning this breakup is not about a "you're not that desperate" mantra. Motivation is only going to take you so far. It's about rewiring the faulty circuitry of desperation by putting yourself, your happiness, and your mental health first. Not just for a few minutes after you put this book down but in the moments where it feels like the most painful and impossible thing to do. It's about staying on your White Horse (and reaping the long-term benefits of doing so) when all you want is to feel the instant gratification of reaching out, responding, retaliating, and reacting.

You are so much better than what your desperation is trying to get you to do.

Yes, you know that your ex is toxic and you are no longer addicted to crumbs, but this just isn't fair. It feels like the tables have turned. When you first got together, he told you that you were too good for him. He said that you turned him on more than anyone he's ever been with. But now, he looks much happier than he ever was with you. And no matter how toxic you know he is, this makes the pain even more unbearable (and moving on seems impossible). Why does he get to be so happy when he's the one who screwed you over? *Did any of it even matter to him?* You're desperate to know.

> **When you are willing to do anything to get a reaction, a response, or an explanation from your ex, *you lower your own value* in his eyes. He gets confirmation that the abuse you are willing to endure is not only limitless but that you are only to be taken *for granted*, never seriously.**

I know how happy he made you, and I know how special the moments were. But you can't just focus ONLY on the parts that exacerbate delusion, all while turning a blind eye to the nonnegotiable red flags that make a mutual relationship impossible.

You're not that desperate.

There is an analogy I love from James Altucher in the book he coauthored, *The Power of No*: "When you have a tiny, tiny piece of crap in your soup, it doesn't matter how much more water you pour in and how many more spices you put on top. There's crap in your soup." I'm going to expand on this and substitute soup for a smoothie because I love smoothies.

Imagine being served a smoothie with the most in season and fresh ingredients in it. Now imagine that a small piece of bird poop was put in the blender with all of those organic fruits and vegetables. If I told you not to drink the smoothie, would you be fighting me? Would you be defending the nutritional value of each and every ingredient in it? Would you be arguing that the bird poop in the smoothie was only "a small piece" and that you "can't even taste it"? Would you be chugging that smoothie down?

I highly doubt it.

But that's what you're doing here. You're scared to accept what your intuition already knows: that no matter how incredible all of the other "ingredients" are on their own, the presence of toxicity disqualifies them from being healthy for you.

I talk to people every day who are going through a breakup where they gave their all to a toxic partner. They tell me how incredible their ex was in the beginning; they thought they had found their soulmate.

But then it takes a very sad and ugly turn.

They go on to tell me how they found out they were being lied to, cheated on, and manipulated for months on end after the honeymoon phase wore off. They blame themselves for everything and are convinced that they must have "done something" to make their ex take advantage of their kindness and "change" all of a sudden.

After telling me every detail and describing their ex as manipulative, dishonest, abusive, and incapable of an adult relationship, many understandably break down in tears. But it's not for the reasons you would think.

- *"Can you believe* she did this?"

- "I'm never going to find someone like him again."

- "What am I going to do without him?"

- "How can I get her back?"

- "You don't understand, Natasha. He made mistakes, but he was so chivalrous in the beginning. I'll never find anyone with looks and a personality like his."

This is *after* telling me how much of a disloyal, selfish asshole their ex ended up being. And although I can empathize because I have so been there, here are my answers:

- "Yes. At this point, it's very believable that she did this. I'm not shocked. You've basically told me that you found something with feathers, quacking in a pond, and can't believe it's a duck. I'm not surprised that it's a duck."

- "You're right. Let's hope you never find someone like him again—*that's the whole point.*"

- "You know what you're going to do without him? Much BETTER."

- "She will 'come back' (get curious) the moment you feel nothing when you think of her. Indifference happens when you have the discipline, every day, to compassionately replace emotional nostalgia with a reminder of the disrespectful behavior you've *already been* on the receiving end of."

- "Although it's great to appreciate chivalry, good looks, and a winning personality, all you have is a chivalrous, good-looking liar with a great personality who cheats. *How is this attractive?* Would you introduce your younger self to this man? Would you want your best friend or a family member to date someone like him?"

You can feel heartbroken over being taken for granted, used, and abused. But wondering how you're going to carry on without a toxic ex because you're convinced that who he was, in the beginning, is who he *really* is?

Again, you're not that desperate.

It's like someone just told you you're cancer-free, and you're crying because you don't know how you're going to live without cancer! It's okay to be heartbroken over what your body went through during the cancer treatments; how it robbed you of time and memories with your loved ones that you'll never get back. But crying about not having cancer is a straight-up denial of the truth— just so you can hold on to the psychological familiarity of being a cancer patient—*no matter how unhealthy it is and how much it takes away from your life.*

The truth really does set you free because it turns you into an emotional entrepreneur. It's an egoic delusion that keeps you trapped in mediocrity, avoidant of reality, and always looking for others to employ you.

Your ex won't come back in the way you're hoping he will (and even then, it will be selfish, not self*less*) until you've truly written him off. Until you no longer give a flying fuck about him and all the baggage he comes with.

You have the ability right now to act on your allergy to toxicity, just like I did with my allergy to gluten in Chapter 6. You can cut your ex off.

I know it's easier to focus on the high of independent moments, but *aren't you disgusted* with the bigger picture here? *Can you believe* what you, your friends, and your family KNOW you've put up with? Aren't you *pissed off* that you're still pedestaling this idiot and stalking his every move after how much he has humiliated you? That you've wasted energy on a man who was never worth it to begin with and aged yourself from all the stress this has caused? Doesn't this make you angry?

You don't need to avoid anger. It's a much more productive emotion than hopelessness and a normal part of the grieving process. With anger, you can actually *do something*. The only time anger becomes toxic is when you bottle it in and don't express it. Or when you act on it in dangerous and destructive ways. Most people think that they need to express their anger to their ex and mutual friends. This isn't a good idea because it makes you look like you don't have a life of your own. It also drains you of your power.

You need to get so angry and fed up that you no longer care to engage.

What got me off the ruminating, the shifting between wanting cheap revenge and blaming myself was understanding that both me AND my ex were in pain and suffering. I realized just how unhappy he had to be with himself to treat me the way that he did. And how unhappy *I* had to be with *myself* to tolerate it, to not be able to own the mistakes I made in our relationship, and to avoid reality at all costs.

At that moment, I stopped wanting to be heard, be right, and "win." I stopped with the one-upmanship. And I realized that the actual "win" was the nontoxic relationship I now had with myself as a result of identifying (and getting away from) the toxic one I had with him.

The best way to get to this place is to stop. Stop trying to educate, enlighten, parent, and exonerate your ex into being the partner and "friend" you deserve. Be the friend to YOURSELF that you truly deserve. Of course, it will still hurt, but you'll be able to let him own his own behavior.

Your peace will be restored only when you choose to prioritize it.

You've already proven that there isn't anything you can't survive. Your heart is still beating, isn't it? Allow your anger to be the nail in the coffin of your old, passive identity (that we killed in Chapter 1) and the fuel for your unfuckwithability going forward. Allow anger to preserve your emotional intelligence when your triggers command you to "get angry" in a way that everyone else can and does. Set yourself apart from the pack by allowing anger to be the fuel for a better you, a better life, and meeting a better man.

I know it's tough because your own eyes and ears have experienced your ex actually *being* everything that he was in the beginning. And you worry about him consistently being that guy with someone new. But when someone has been shittier than they are kind and honest, more careless than they are caring, and more selfish than they are empathetic, why on earth would you think that you were powerful enough to be **the sole cause** of these discrepancies?

Even though you made your own mistakes in the relationship (which you need to own but not overly blame yourself for; relationships are a two-way street), NO ONE is powerful enough to scare, smother, love, irritate, and communicate the humanity and integrity *out* of someone else.

There is no need to assume he's a better man just because it creates the certainty you need to perpetuate the false belief that you are not enough. Take a look in the mirror and ask yourself:

Have I FINALLY had enough?

Will I protect my younger self?

Will I become everything that my ex never was and never will be?

Will I let him own his own behavior?

Will I run out of shits to give when it comes to the opinions of others?

Will I be the woman who knows when someone is disrespecting her and actually *acts* on that knowledge instead of feeling like I have to put on a detailed presentation and explain myself to a man who cannot emotionally see or hear?

Will I be the dynamic character in my own life story instead of the guest-starring doormat in everyone else's?

Stop telling yourself that he changed.

There was no "change." He misrepresented himself, and as time passed, he got more comfortable. You then got to see WHAT he really is: *toxic*.

Your ex presented himself as a bar of solid, twenty-four-carat gold and ended up tarnishing into a turd. Just because the gold coating faded and you're now left with a turd, that isn't an indicator of your lack of value or that the turd will "change back." It's proof that it was never solid to begin with; it was full of shit! And you need to FLUSH. Immediately.

This man lacks character. And character is not just about matching words with actions. It's about being able to match those actions with consistent patterns over time.

He came on strong and ended up *revealing*. He didn't come in emotionally intelligent and end up "changing."

This breakup is testing your resolve in ways that nothing ever has before. It is now time to overcome everything you've never been able to not give into.

YOU'RE NOT THAT DESPERATE TO FALL FOR THE "I MISS YOU."

If you respond at all to the chain yank of an "I miss you," you're communicating that it's all right to keep treating you like the fallback that you have no problem being.

When a toxic ex sends an "I miss you" message, it's because he wants his all-access pass back. He misses having access to *all that you provided*. He misses the you who tirelessly tried to get him to see your worth. So he sends out an "I miss you" to take your temperature and see if your self-esteem is still nonexistent. It's no skin off his back! He has everything to gain, and you, quite literally, have everything to lose.

When you were in the relationship with your ex, you always felt like you had to be giving or doing something to "keep" him and his attention. He has proven to be selfish and emotionally disconnected, which means that he misses everything you DID for his ego, not everything that you ARE.

He misses the old you that listened to all of his problems. The insecure, empathetic-to-a-fault you who made everything about him, helped him and supported him in every which way. He misses how quick you were to excuse the inexcusable, try to make sense of the nonsensical, defend the indefensible, "forgive," and "start over."

He misses the doormat you *were*, not the person you *are*.

Another reason for the "I miss you" chain yank is because he realizes that the grass is not greener. You treated him like a dignitary, but the "greener grass" he was hoping for just sees him as the commoner that he is.

You may get an "I miss you" or something along those lines if he's bored, heard that you're dating, are happy, or if you've completely cut him off. If you're not begging to get back together or reacting the way he expected you to, it will *dismantle* his ego.

Bottom line: We are attracted to people who ultimately affirm the belief system that we have about ourselves. You no longer believe that your ex is something that he has *consistently proven* he isn't because you no longer believe that you are everything you *never were*—worthless, weak, defective, and unlovable.

And just like the man you're missing does not exist, the *access* he's missing no longer exists in his relational world. Your dignity is making sure of that.

You deserve so much more than someone who "misses" you from afar while continuing to shit their emotional shorts.

YOU'RE NOT THAT DESPERATE TO CONFUSE ABANDONMENT ISSUES WITH HIS VALUE.

When our fear of abandonment is triggered, we will do anything to avoid having to experience the trauma of feeling alone. Instead of acknowledging this as our own issue, we confuse the desperation that we are feeling for our ex having increased value. How unglued we become is then, in true romantic comedy fashion, a symptom of how "worth it" he must be instead of how much *more* worth it we *are*.

YOU'RE NOT THAT DESPERATE TO "JUST BE FRIENDS."

Never demote yourself to a "friend" or fuck buddy, ever. The only way you can be friends with an ex is if time has passed, THEY

ARE NOT TOXIC, you've both moved on, and you *both* have zero romantic feelings for each other. In any other situation, it's a terrible idea.

If you think about it, your ex was never a true friend to you. He treated you much worse than a friend. Expecting him to be a better "friend" to you now that you're no longer in a romantic relationship with him is a complete waste of time and an insult to your intelligence.

Whenever you try to stay friends with a toxic ex, it's because you don't want to come across as weak, you don't want to come across as immature, and you're not quite ready to completely cut everything off. It's scary, it's painful, and you miss him. You'd rather have him as a lousy "friend" than not have him at all.

The problem is, when you decide to be friends with an ex who is toxic, he doesn't get to experience any consequences for what he did and put you through. You guys are "friends"! And you're still in his life. He won't suddenly understand what he did wrong and how incredible you are by you being his friend. All he will see is a woman whose desperation has dissolved her self-respect.

Consequences for hurtful behavior come from dignified *action*, not fake friendships.

YOU'RE NOT THAT DESPERATE TO THINK HIS REBOUND IS THE REAL DEAL.

Rebound relationships are a specific type of toxic relationship that form quickly after (or sometimes before) a breakup. They are adult security blankets composed of 0 percent cotton and 100 percent avoidance of guilt, responsibility, accountability, and reality.

When I was toxic, I wouldn't get into a rebound relationship because I was suddenly "a better person" after breaking up with someone who was too good for me to begin with. It was simply the easiest way to avoid having to deal with myself. It was more about mending my bruised ego than it EVER was about healthily moving on.

Your ex getting into a new relationship right away is never about you. I know you're wondering, "How could he not care?" "How could he do that to me and embarrass me like this?" "What does she have that I don't?" This man cannot see outside of his impulsive and egoic needs. Remember, it's all about *external* validation for him. Nothing is ever as real, premeditated, and planned as your fears (and social media) are trying to convince you.

She may have things that you don't have. But you have the one thing that she CLEARLY does not yet have: 20/20 vision when it comes to toxicity, performative bullshit, and selfishness.

Rebound relationships are distractions. Period. The reason that they usually fail is because of the very distraction they provide. As long as your ex is distracted, he never has to think, feel, or take responsibility. Unlike you, he doesn't have the courage to be alone and self-reflect before moving on. He's still the same selfish person in the same nonmutual relationship.

Someone who lies to and cheats on you will lie to and cheat on the next one. And it doesn't matter how amazing his new partner is either. Ultimately, no one can make anyone change out of being who they are at the core.

These relationships don't last (and even if they do, they're not high-quality relationships) because no evolution or change takes place on your ex's end. Even if the rebound results in a marriage proposal, there is no healing and no dealing—remember that. It's very hard to form an intimate and connected relationship with someone when the relationship was either built on deception or has happened right after a previous (and toxic) relationship has ended.

Your ex is taking the easy way out in life, and ironically, his life will end up becoming increasingly difficult. You chose to do the hard work with every odd against you. And you will reap the benefits of emotional entrepreneurism for the rest of your life. Don't give up on yourself now.

YOU'RE NOT THAT DESPERATE TO INTERPRET APOLOGIES AND WITHHOLD FORGIVENESS.

With toxic people, "I'm sorry" usually means, "I shouldn't have done what I did because now I'm no longer getting my needs met. Can you please reset our relationship with your forgiveness so I can stop feeling the way I do?" It will never mean "I'm remorseful," "I've changed," "I realize how I've hurt you, and I feel terrible about it. I want to make things right."

When someone is genuinely sorry, they will respect your newly adjusted boundaries with awareness of the pain that their behavior caused. They won't push you to forgive, nor will they pressure you into accepting their apology or even acknowledging it. They'll have confidence in their character, honesty, and integrity. And they'll let you be. They won't "apologize" to you and then punish you for not forgiving them the way their ego needs you to. This is because their apology is about acknowledging *you*, not inflating your just-as-fragile ego so that access to their supply can be regained.

When you no longer operate from your ego, "apologies" like this will do nothing for you. You'll shrug your shoulders at the non-sense, move on with your day, and be thankful that you know what true forgiveness *really* means.

If your toxic ex ever apologizes to you, he will most likely be doing so just to hear back from you. He may even throw in a "this is the last time you will ever hear from me" to up the ante.

He knows that if anyone who has two emotionally intelligent brain cells to rub together "gets to you," or even worse, if YOU get back to *yourself* and realize who the fuck you are, he won't be able to get you back into a transactionship. And the only way to get you back is to do what he's always done to keep you locked in: manipulate you. Except this time, it's through "self-reflection," convenient "realizations," and "apologies."

Toxic exes use apologies to evade guilt on their end. Since they're all about image, they don't want to look like the creep that they are. So they apologize. This has nothing to do with an awareness of hurting you and breaking your trust. It has to do with how they look to the outside world. Apologies are also used to see if you're still so desperate that you'll appreciate the crumb of an "apology" enough to start a "friendship" and be a bench-warming option the next time their ego takes a hit.

An apology from a toxic ex is not something that you ever have to respond to if you don't want to.

I used to have a really hard time with forgiveness. Toxic people view forgiveness as condoning their behavior and a relational reset, but it's far from that. Forgiveness has nothing to do with letting go of your hopes and dreams (this comes from gaining *perspective*, which takes *time*). It has nothing to do with forgetting what happened or things going back to normal. Forgiveness is adjusted boundaries. That's *it*. If someone hurts you, betrays your trust, and is disloyal, you adjust your boundaries accordingly and move the fuck on. You don't try to pull an apology out of someone who had no problem doing what they did to you. Repeatedly.

Forgiveness is adjusting your boundaries in light of accepting who someone has proven themselves to be.

It's not about hanging on to the man he was when you were on vacation last year and allowing that hologram to dilute your sense of reality. It's about accepting *what* he is today (toxic). It's also about forgiving yourself. I've forgiven myself by adjusting my boundaries with *my own* toxicity.

Listen, you will eventually recover from this. It will get better; I want you to know that. If you give up now, you will never win this breakup. You have to keep going. Take it minute by minute and then hour by hour. There *will* come a day when you hear your ex's name and feel nothing. Every detail that you're hanging on to right now will be forgotten. You'll be living a life that's so incredible that you don't have the capacity to believe it in this moment, but you will get there.

I haven't just "bounced back" after going through difficult times and unwanted breakups. I've done unimaginable damage to my physical health as a result of heartbreak. I got stress-induced vertigo and very intense panic attacks because I couldn't let go. I'd wake up in the middle of the night, soaked in a cold sweat with swollen eyes, wondering why I couldn't just die. So believe me when I say, I see you. I feel you, and I understand your pain.

But I know the day will come when you realize you don't need to keep hanging on to the memory of a man who does not exist. You never needed him to complete you—you needed your younger self.

You'll look back on this time with so much self-respect and gratitude because you would never appreciate the life you built (and the people in it) to the extent that you do, without knowing just how bad it can be.

You will be living happily on your own terms because you fought for every bit of this peace and success.

You will be giving your pain a purpose and helping others out of toxicity that you will never again find yourself in because you can no longer find it *within*.

You will follow through with the promises that you made to yourself because you are now able to observe instead of blindly invest.

You will also realize the GIFT that your ex gave you. Without him, there would be no "us," no me and you. We found each other because we wanted more. And our bond can never be broken.

You will forgive yourself and one day come back to this book—not to reread it but to give it to someone who needs it because you no longer do.

When you choose to forgive yourself, you'll stop worrying about what your ex thinks and start living your best life. It's infectious, it's attractive, and it's powerful. When you forgive yourself, part of this is accepting that some people will disappear from your life when they realize that you no longer have a lack of boundaries and self-love to feed off. Others will turn against you because your independence highlights their *dependence* on your fear of their rejection. And that's totally fine. These are not your people. Let them go. Forgive them and move on. Focus on those who love and support you—starting with your younger self.

Forgive your ex *for* your younger self. It's a favor to her, not him. You don't need to make an announcement to everyone, post quotes about forgiveness on social media, or tell your ex that you forgive him.

Stay on your White Horse. Adjust your boundaries in silence and move accordingly.

No one that ever wins ANYTHING tells the audience or, even worse, the *opposition* what their next move is. If you keep focusing on every single injustice, it will trap you in your pain and keep you in a state of reactivity. But if you accept what is and vow to protect yourself from future exposure, you will eventually be released from these shackles.

You are your own savior, champion, and best friend, your own Knight in Shining Armor.

We all have the ability to be our greatest relationship. Once we can tap into the unconditional self-love that we have for our younger selves, everything becomes tipped in our favor because we are no longer fueled by outside opinions, people, and possessions.

We are fueled from *within*.

And when you are fueled from within, *no one* can take that away.

I know how much you miss your ex, but he is not the irreplaceable one. YOU are.

He doesn't yet know the strength you have rebuilt, the White Horse you are riding, the demons you have slain…

And the desperation you have now overcome.

Part 3

WINNING
YOUR
BREAKUP

10

Breaking *UP*, Not Down

Everything you are feeling and experiencing right now means that there is a big difference between what you know you deserve and what you actually got. *Do you know how powerful this realization is?* You *know* you got short-changed. You know that you want to break *UP* into a life you can call your own, instead of breaking *down* into your fears, succumbing to your insecurities, and validating not only your ex but anyone who ever made you feel small enough to tolerate what you no longer will.

Yes, you got knocked down. You were hungrier for a crumb than you were willing to have limits. You questioned your worth and your reality. You allowed desperation to prosecute your intuition and the fear of abandonment to obliterate your boundaries. You were humiliated at every turn, lied to, used, abused, and spit out.

But you didn't know what to believe, so you gave second chances that were never earned, only half-heartedly explained.

And as much as it doesn't feel like you'll ever get over this breakup, the worst is behind you now.

> *You* **are the one who needed a second chance, and that's what you've been given.**

Deep down, you know that your ex cannot stand on both relational, emotional, and empathetic feet. And because of this, there's still a part of you that no matter how heartbroken, *knows* he is unable to be in a relationship with anyone beyond a very superficial level, let alone be capable of reciprocating love, loyalty, and honesty.

> **The only people who are capable of a return on investment (a mutual relationship) are those who don't have to rely on the investments of others for their own egoic survival.**

A lion doesn't need to come into a room and say, "Hey, guys, just so you know, I'm a lion. I've got sharp claws, I can roar like none other, oh and guess what else? I'm also king of the jungle. Bow down!" All a lion has to do for people to know he's a lion is just be. That's what kings do.

Your joker of an ex is a house cat wearing a fake lion mane. And who cares if other people think they're in the presence of a lion?

YOU know the truth, and that's more than enough.

Just think about how insecure someone has to feel to operate on such a delusional level. You are so much smarter than believing in a man who refuses to hear his own meows and instead gets his kicks off of making you feel like you're just deaf to a "real" roar. You are so much more than anyone who could not love you, value you, be honest with you, or see your worth.

From now on, you won't have to try so hard. I spent the first twenty-four years of my life desperate for people to notice me, like me, and include me. If only I could be good enough to gain their validation and approval. I tried embarrassingly hard to be liked, loved, and accepted because I couldn't like, love, and accept myself. Everything that was meant to be an *experience* to learn and grow from, I adopted as an irrefutable definition of my worth. This is why I could never move on or reach indifference after betrayal. I couldn't stop circling the emotional drain because I was in denial and betraying myself at every turn.

You will never reach indifference until you have the courage to get real with yourself and stop pretending. Stop posting quotes that translate a "hidden message" you want to passively get across to a man who doesn't know his emotional ass from his emotional elbow. BE the message. Deliver it through how you *live* your life, not how you want him to think you do.

How would you feel about this breakup if you were diagnosed with a terminal condition tomorrow? Would you continue to stalk your ex and stress over him at the expense of your health? Or would you start taking care of yourself and only give your time and energy to those who were worthy of it?

We are all terminal; our lives are guaranteed to end in our physical death. And if you are lucky, in a few decades (that will go by faster than you could ever imagine), everyone you know will be six feet under or ashes.

Take a moment to let that sink in.

Everything you're obsessing over right now will not matter.

What *will* matter is that you went for it, that you valued your time by honoring your condition instead of dishonoring it. That you had your own back, built a life of your own, and made memories in the process that no one can ever take away.

Do you really want to be at the end of your life, riddled with regret because you lived every day on your knees, pedestaling this lunatic and destroying your destiny? Or do you want to look back and *know* you were a dynamic character? That you got up in a way NO ONE saw coming when you were knocked to the ground and left for dead. That you actually lived a life worth living. That your success took up permanent residency in the minds of those who broke and doubted you, but you could care less either way.

Don't you want to know what it's like to experience THAT level of emotional freedom in your lifetime? You CAN, and you're on your way. This is not the time to give in to fear. Don't go back to the pacifier of fantasy land just because it's the only place that your ex can exist in your mind as an emotionally intelligent adult.

Stay *on* your White Horse and *in* reality.

When it comes to relationships, the level to which you deceive yourself will always mirror the toleration you have for others deceiving you.

Everyone who is massively successful (emotionally, relationally, professionally, and financially) hits rock bottom at some point in their lives. They went through an isolation period where they felt their way through every ounce of their pain, shut out the noise, and came out on the other end a warrior who was never the same.

You need to decide who's more important here—your ex *or* your younger self? I can't say, "Your ex or yourself" because you've already chosen him over the adult that you are. But would you really choose him over your younger self?

I want you to imagine that you are standing in the middle of a cold and foggy street. On one side, your ex is standing. On the other side, you at five years old. Both are looking back at you, counting on you to choose them.

Your ex is getting impatient, but he's certain that you'll choose him. He checks his phone to see who's texted and starts making plans for the weekend.

Your younger self is looking all around and bouncing her little legs. She tries to hold back tears from falling and starts to shiver. She's scared and isn't sure that she'll be chosen because she never has been.

I want you to tell me, right now, *who would you choose*?

Would you run to your ex and abandon that little girl? Could you live with yourself knowing you did that to her?

I know how much you want to go to your ex's side of the street. You feel like you were born to love him, and you still can. I'm not asking you to stop loving the man whom you thought existed (which is the same reason why many restrictive diets fail). I'm asking you to love that little girl *more*. She has no voice, no one to call, no home, and no one to protect her and keep her warm.

No one but YOU.

If you love that little girl *more* than you love your ex and choose to go to her side of the street, you will never again come to the relational table starving, depleted, desperate, and defeated. And at that point, you'll no longer care to get your ex back (which is usually when he'll circle back around). You'll be too busy, too plugged into your own life to waste your time.

Have you ever noticed when you're really busy, you don't care as much about keeping up with the drama, reacting to idiots, or getting revenge? When someone hurts you, of course it still hurts, but because you have so much going on in your own life, you can bounce back much easier and not hold on to resentment. **You may burn bridges if the other person's actions provided the matches, but you don't hold grudges.** There's only so much time in the day, and you have only so much energy to give to every little thing.

The funny thing is, that mindset is what ends up *destroying* toxic people like your ex. It isn't your reactions and explanations that get to him. It's you having better things to do than feel obligated to emotionally educate a grown man. You're not into humiliating and emasculating him; you're better than that. Plus, he already does a great job of doing it to himself! He doesn't need you jumping on the bandwagon.

Your indifference levels the playing field here because your ex expects you to be just as invested in him, his whereabouts, and his life *after* the breakup as you were in the relationship. The fact that you've totally unplugged from him and now plugged into a life of your own is too sobering of a reality to be faced with. He can't believe that you now know who the fuck you are, that you're building a better life and becoming a better, more successful, evolved, attractive, and aware person *after* him.

NO ONE wants to feel like they were nothing more than a launching pad.

Your ex's actions have given you no choice but to prove just how high you can fly above the lows of his bullshit.

When you make the executive decision to cut a toxic ex off, this makes him realize that *he* is the one who is at a loss, not you. It *dignifiedly* puts him in his place.

Every time he's tried to call your bluff, your silence has informed him that you will choose peace of mind over the ambiguity of amateur hour every damn time. People like your ex count on you getting off your White Horse and reacting to their obnoxiousness. They count on you to always be desperate for and appreciative of crumbs. Their egoic survival is dependent on it.

Think of your favorite public figure and how much hate they get on social media. Are they replying to every hateful comment? No. They have too much going on in their own life! In fact, the people who hate on them end up looking like fools, like they have nothing better to do than hate on someone whom they apparently despise so much, they know everything about (and stalk their every move on social media). Meanwhile, the public figure is busy living their life, focusing only on those who support and uplift them.

Right now, you may feel like you don't have a life independent of your ex, and that's okay. In a world where you can't control much of anything, you will always have total control over these three things:

1. What you put in your body.

2. How much you move your body.

3. Whether you let your emotions dictate your actions (by getting off your White Horse and reacting to them).

Boredom will make this breakup infinitely harder. If you have nothing to do, make sure that at the very least, you're focusing on eating healthy and moving your body. When I was going through one of the toughest breakups of my life, I would go to the gym or go on a long run *right after* getting off work. And I started eating healthier as a result. I was working out so hard (but being healthy about it, not reckless) that I was so exhausted when I did have downtime, I didn't care about stalking and obsessing as much as I used to. I'd watch a show on TV and unwind. It was really difficult at first, but after a while, it got easier.

As I got physically stronger, my mental and emotional strength followed suit. I had built back my self-respect because every minute that went by, I knew it was another minute that I fought for my survival and WON. It definitely took time, but having something to put my energy into helped tremendously.

If I would have taken the time to unpack and interpret every single trauma in my past, my present, and in my relationships, I don't know if I would be alive today. This isn't to say that working through trauma isn't beneficial; it definitely is. But building a life of my own not only healed me, but it also got me off the treadmill of obsession and on the road. I was doing the same amount of work but was actually *getting* somewhere this time instead of staying in the same place, trying to unturn every stone and figure out every reason why.

This isn't about escapism or avoidance. It's about using your trauma to build the kind of success that you could never have if you didn't have such a burning desire to get rid of the "doormat" title from your relational résumé.

There is so much more to your story than this breakup being The End for you.

This is not your cue to break down. It's your one chance to break UP.

BREAKING UP RULE #1: REDEFINE REJECTION

The only way that rejection of any kind can destroy you is if you've already rejected your younger self and chosen to go to your ex's side of the street. How you deal with rejection is tied to how much of a life you have independent of the person or entity rejecting you and how much you love and protect your younger self.

You know that your ex isn't worthy of your second chances, replies, and explanations. This makes you feel even more depressed and confused, though, because how could someone so disrespectful and dishonest be rejecting you, *especially* after you gave so much? If anything, you should have been the one rejecting him!

And as terrible as this sounds, after almost every breakup I've gone through, I've thought, "How could he not at least *continue* to take advantage of me? He's not even trying to keep *using* me!" There are few things worse than feeling like you failed *as a doormat*, like you weren't even worthwhile enough to keep being used.

But you need to remember that rejection is never personal when it comes to toxic exes; it's about them. Your ex is rejecting having to be a grown man instead of "THE" man. He's rejecting the idea of becoming an evolutionary being. He's rejecting having to be honest, accountable, and responsible for anything other than inflating his ego. Your relationship got to a point where he knew things were being (reasonably) asked and expected of him.

And he just couldn't deliver.

Never ask anyone who broke you why they rejected you.

They won't be able to answer, and ultimately, your ex won't be able to provide these relational necessities to *anyone*, no matter how convincing he makes it seem on social media. The only way that a relationship could work with this man is if he's in total control and you don't have a problem with being used, lied to, abused, and sidelined. Things like honesty, maturity, and empathy are simply not part of his psychological vocabulary.

He did not reject you. YOU are simply rejecting what is toxic to your mental health.

BREAKING UP RULE #2: CLEAN UP YOUR CONTRADICTIONS

There is a popular term called catfishing. It basically means to get into communication (and eventually an intimate relationship) with someone (who has no idea they're being conned) via a totally fabricated online persona. Now I am going to ask you a very important question, and I want you to be completely honest with yourself and me.

Would you ever put up with being catfished?

If you had met your ex online and his pictures were of a completely different man than who he is in person, *what would you have done?* Would you have taken it personally?

I'll tell you what you would have done:

You would have been so disturbed that you would have turned around and never looked back. You would not be calling your family and friends to ask for advice on how you should proceed. And you definitely would not think that this was about you. The betrayal would hurt, yes, but the level of deception would propel you into action.

You would accept that this man is deranged and that it clearly has nothing to do with you. He would have done this to anyone. You would never try to be "better" or "good enough" in hopes of resurrecting the hot businessman in the photos from the one in front of you who is happily unemployed, has abandoned his hygiene, and is living with his mother. There would be no choice but to accept that the man in front of you is a completely different person than the one in the photos and *act* on that acceptance.

The same needs to be applied when you are *emotionally* catfished. Stop trying to resurrect the man that never was from the boy whose emotional intelligence makes Peter Pan look like Confucius.

Yes, there is such a thing as emotional catfishing. And it's much more prevalent than physical catfishing, which is so widely publicized that there have been movies and television shows dedicated to it.

Although you were not physically catfished in this relationship that you are now breaking *UP* from, you were *emotionally* catfished. And the only reason you're still swimming in denial is that you are overvaluing the superficial—things that you can't grow old with because they change and fade with time. These things do not constitute real companionship and loyalty. They constitute image, orgasm if you're lucky, and bravado.

Emotional catfishing can take much longer to reveal itself than physical catfishing does. But why are you allowing your insecurities to make it any less clear to see, any less disturbing to experience, or any less of a red flag deal breaker? Your ex came to the table presenting himself as someone who was relationally ready or competent at the very least. He revealed himself to be a selfish, emotional bum. A bum who made decisions that *came with the risk* of experiencing the kind of reality that your boundaries and dignity are now ensuring he experiences. Remain on your White Horse and let your absence be the consequence.

Clean up this contradiction and also clean up the contradiction that you have with your *own* emotional catfishing. Make the decision now to stop presenting yourself as someone who won't tolerate being a doormat but has the dirt from her ex's emotional boots all over her.

Just like with physical catfishing, emotional catfishing has nothing to do with you and everything to do with the awareness, self-love, and confidence that the catfisher *lacks*.

BREAKING UP RULE #3:
CLOSURE IS A MEAL THAT'S BEST
SELF-MADE AND SELF-SERVED

Right now, you feel like it's your right to get the closure you deserve. And although you've definitely earned that right, you become convinced that there's only one way to get it: via your ex, who has already proven that he cannot be trusted, consistent, communicative, mature, or loyal. You need this man, who has lied to, used, and manipulated you, to NOW *empathetically*, *remorsefully*, and *honestly* fill in the blanks that your own eyes, ears, and intuition already know the answers to.

Do you know how unreasonable this sounds?

> **You will lose every time trying to get closure from a toxic ex.**
> **And in the process of that loss, you will end up giving *his ego* the**
> **reassurance and closure that yours is seeking.**

Having to literally pry the truth out of someone, who had no problem giving you every "version" of it, is not sexy. Neither is translating through your actions that although *you know* he is incapable of being honest, you believe that he'll somehow be emotionally intelligent enough to give it to you for the sake of you needing "closure" now that it's over.

Even if your ex admitted to everything you ever wanted, even if he told you how much he regretted what he did and how sorry he was, trust me when I say that it would not make you feel any better. You would feel worse because it would mess with your mind even more. Not only would you have a hard time trusting those words after so much bullshit and betrayal, but it should never take someone losing you to deem you worthy of basics like respect and honesty.

I've tried everything to forget toxic exes whom I could not get closure from—mantras, hypnosis, meditation, rebound relationships, one-night stands, going out with friends, cleanses, dancing the night away, being set up on dates, blocking/unblocking, following/unfollowing, tagging/untagging, new hairstyles, "ridding-my-life-of-toxicity" quote posting...you name it. Nothing worked. In the end, I just hated myself even more. **This left me no choice but to pedestal someone whose absence I was more fearful of feeling than the toxicity I was afraid of** *accepting.*

Acceptance is scary. Once you accept who someone has revealed themselves to be, you then have to bring the focus back to yourself.

You have to break *UP* from the mindset that tolerated this kind of treatment in the first place.

Remember everything your ex did, how it made you feel, and allow *that* to be your closure. It IS possible. Allow the painful memories that can't get erased to be the answers in and of themselves.

You will never be able to accept what is until you recognize what isn't.

Same with forgetting. The more you focus on forgetting, the more you'll remember. And you will never be able to forget what you need to until you make an effort to remember what you have to. This is what true closure is all about.

What you're doing now—thinking that you weren't good enough, blaming yourself, and buying into the baseless belief that your ex has changed (he hasn't)—is so much more difficult than what I am suggesting. All I am asking is that you remember what your own eyes, ears, gut, and instinct have *already witnessed* and been exposed to in real time.

Whether you hear from him or not, the woman that a toxic ex looks back on as "The One That Got Away" is the one who, *through her silence, absence, indifference, and living life on her own terms,* says:

"*Closure?* I don't need it from you. What you chose to do, what you chose not to do, and your predictable patterns are all I needed to listen to. Your words mean nothing, and mine won't be wasted on you any longer. I don't care about your explanations, sympathy-mongering excuses, and your newly discovered realizations. I don't care about whom you're dating and how well you're treating her or how much she's benefiting from all of your 'learned lessons.' You will never get a reaction out of me because you can't fuck with me anymore. I may be hurt, I may be upset, but I have my own set of eyes, ears, and most importantly, I have my own back and my own White Horse. I love me, and I chose *her* side of the street. I am my own priority. I don't care about you thinking that you won or feeling powerful because only someone who feels extremely power*less* could operate the way you do. And this isn't about you. It's about me. And I'm finally free. Have a nice life."

BREAKING UP RULE #4: TOSS THE LOSS

As long as you view this as a "loss," you will continue to break down, not UP. When toxic relationships become a pattern, you are no longer a victim to the toxicity of others, nor are you a victim to your own level of toxicity that allowed you to put up with it from others in the first place. You become a volunteer. This is your chance to get out of the recycle bin of victim to volunteer and start going from victim to vict*or*.

The bad news about being in a relationship with a toxic person is that you are in it. The good news about *not* being in a relationship with them anymore is that it's never a loss. In life, we are faced with loss every day, but part of being an emotional entrepreneur is being able to identify which losses are actually *wins*.

As we discussed in Chapter 7, it is not possible to lose a toxic person. You can never lose a toxic person, just like you can never lose crap in the toilet once you flush. You can only gain a clean, crap-free toilet. There are no losses in this situation. Has there ever been a toilet that you've looked back at and regretted flushing? I don't think so. Stop stirring the crap in the toilet just because it reminds you of the great meal that once was. Stop giving yourself a license to cry over the smell that you are choosing to perpetuate. The meal wasn't that great anyway. You were just *that* hungry.

Remember, it's all right to grieve the loss of the man you thought existed as long as you firmly root yourself in the knowingness that he is not subject to resurrection. He *never* existed.

You were not the pad that launched him into "greatness." It's time to let your indifference and success show just how much of a launching pad he and his dysfunction really are.

And congratulations—you just broke *UP*.

11

How to Feel Turned OFF
by the Thought
of Your Ex

The moment you decide to choose your younger self and build a life of your own, that is the moment your ex will want you to choose him. The more you stay on your White Horse and enforce standards that are backed by solid boundaries, the more your ex will either...

Shit his emotional shorts even more in light of such dynamic and unforeseen action.

OR...

He will have no choice but to be humbled and respect the fact that you became someone he can only pretend to be. Your dignity and nonreactivity (staying on your White Horse) have made it obvious that he's a little leaguer in what is now the Major Leagues.

And since he's so competitive and always has to "win," he won't know what to do other than pretend to be able to keep up. This is sad but fortunately no longer your problem.

The problem is, no matter how aware you are of your ex's toxicity and how committed you now are to your younger self, there's still a part of you that feels attracted to him. I know; you're ashamed of it. I get it. You shouldn't still be attracted to him at this point, but you are. And it's okay because that's what this chapter is for: to learn how to become turned OFF by *the thought of him* whenever emotional nostalgia comes knocking.

Of all the emotions that we feel as humans, one of my absolute favorites is disgust. I don't wake up every day and hope to feel disgusted, but the reason I appreciate this emotion so much is that it's the only emotion that I, personally, have not been able to feel while desperate.

Desperation is an emotion that nearly cost me my life, which is why I had an entire chapter dedicated to extinguishing it in this book. I've been in love and desperate, scared and desperate, insecure and desperate, angry and desperate, sad and desperate;

I've even been happy and desperate. But I've never been disgusted and desperate.

Disgust has been one of the most liberating emotions for me. I can feel completely powerless in a situation, but the moment disgust kicks in, all bets are off.

Desperation is blinding. And it can be a very dangerous emotion. It will rob you of your unique personality, health, identity, happiness, and destiny. I've ignored my own morals, reality, and sense of loyalty—all while in the grip of desperation. So any environment that desperation *cannot* thrive in, I'm all for.

> **Disgust is what I refer to as a "light switch" emotion. Once you're disgusted by someone or something, there's no going back. The lights are either on, or they're off. There is no "halfway" point here. Just like the lights can never be partially on, you can never be partially disgusted.**

I don't drink alcohol anymore, but one night, when I was in college, I went out and had too many drinks, all containing raspberry-flavored vodka. I ended up getting very sick that night and couldn't keep anything down. Now, here's the interesting thing about that night:

To this day, if I so much as *smell* raspberry-flavored vodka, it will induce a gag reflex.

That night, my body was so physically disgusted that over ONE DECADE LATER, it will *still* induce a gag reflex upon *smelling* (not even consuming!) the raspberry-flavored vodka.

Isn't it incredible what our body can hold on to and remember, just to protect us from more trauma? Our *emotional* body is the same way. We just prevent it from helping us at every turn.

I used to wonder how I could be so disgusted by a certain food or drink that years and years down the line, my body would *still* remember and immediately remind me of that disgust. So why couldn't I do this with my relationships?

Is there such thing as an *emotional* gag reflex? And if so, why was I missing one?

I knew that on a superficial level, I could get disgusted. I could go out on a date with a really great guy, and all it took was a dirty toenail, a hair growing out of a small facial mole, bad breath, dandruff, gross table manners or eating habits, etc., and I'd be so disgusted that there was no way I could continue. And it didn't matter how incredible of a person he was either. Once disgust kicked in, it was over. This was odd because I was insecure and desperate to be in a relationship. But once I got disgusted by something superficial, I became liberated and confident enough to walk away! No amount of genuine kindness, emotional availability, maturity, or empathy could get me to turn back around. But (and this is so shameful to admit) if I met a man who lied to me, manipulated me, used me, and was all-around toxic, YET had all of the superficial boxes ticked, disgust would *never* set in.

I learned the hard way that this wasn't because I was born without an emotional gag reflex; we are all born with one. It's because not loving yourself enough to have boundaries will disable your emotional gag reflex from *ever* kicking in.

Humans are afraid of disgust because they know the power of it.

There is absolutely nothing disgusting about giving birth. It is one of the most beautiful experiences in life. I've never given birth (and I am extremely sensitive to those who struggle with infertility), but I've been in the delivery room many times with friends and family members. All of them wanted their partner to be in the room with them, but most of them would not let their partner anywhere near the birth canal.

Why? Because it's disgusting? Well, no.

It's because they know there's the power of seeing something that you just can't unsee. And that's scary.

This breakup has placed you right in front of your ex's birth canal. And no matter how hard you try, you cannot unsee what you've already seen.

You don't need anyone to validate what you've seen; you just need to let go. I know it's scary because once disgust kicks in, there is no going back, but you're not alone here. Surrender to the trust that you have in your own eyes and ears. Accept that you can't unsee what you've seen and allow your emotional gag reflex to kick in because it can and it will.

There is nothing new to see in the past. You are standing right in front of your ex's birth canal, and I am telling you (along with your family and friends who love and believe in you) that it is fucking disgusting.

You don't need to be scared anymore. You don't need to worry that if you turn around for a split second, a rose garden will grow. It won't. And even if it did, trust me when I say, you'll never be able to get the image out of your head that you just can't unsee.

Get disgusted by the misrepresentation. Your ex presented himself as someone that he doesn't have the capacity to be consistently. Isn't that gross? And speaking of capacities, *does it even matter who or what he ends up becoming?* You already know that this man has the capacity to carry out behavior that doesn't coincide with your value system. Even if he does change, *you know what he's **capable** of.* And that knowingness needs to disgust you.

You would never date someone who had been in trouble with the law for abusing animals, would you? If this person told you that he was just "being dumb," that he had a "phase" of kicking puppies and setting kittens on fire, but that was in the past, and he was "all good" now, *what would you do?* Would you date this person? I know I wouldn't!

Yes, of course, we ALL make mistakes and do terrible things that we can learn and grow from. Rehabilitation is possible; I don't want to discredit that. But we also have the right not to want to be with someone, no matter how rehabilitated they are, whose capacities don't align with our *personal* value system. For me, having the capacity to set a helpless animal on fire is so bad that I don't care how rehabilitated this person is; if they were ever even *capable* of that kind of behavior, a relationship of any kind with me just isn't in the cards. Plain and simple.

I cannot tell you what your limits are. Only you know that answer, and of course, anyone can poke holes in ANY analogy I use. There are always exceptions to every little thing, but that is not my concern here. My main concern, with all the love in my heart, is igniting that emotional gag reflex of yours so that you can win this breakup and your ex can rue the day he decided to fuck with you.

What I can tell you is this: Your ex has *shown you* that he has *the capacity* to devalue, deceive, abuse, and disrespect your younger self. HOW is that any worse than kicking a puppy or setting a kitten on fire? *How?*

You have a choice right now. You can look at the photo of your younger self and explain to that little girl why you want to give this loser another chance because "he didn't really mean it." Or you can be a dynamic character who unconditionally loves that child and has her back. You can show her how disgusted you are by that behavior, introduce her to your White Horse, and ride out of the bullshit and into a place of peace together. You can prove to her right now that you unconditionally love her, that under your watch, she is unfuckwithable. It's up to you.

There's also the added layer of betrayal. Your ex has shown you that he's capable of not only justifying betrayal, but *while he was betraying you*, he expected YOU never to betray HIM! How disgusting is that? It's so bad that it's laughable.

How can you still look at a photo of him and be turned on? How can you stomach the disloyalty? The truth is, you can't. Humans are not psychologically or physically built to be in an intimate relationship with a toxic person for the rest of their lives. Our minds and bodies will eventually give out.

All of the happiness that you felt in the relationship with your ex—YOU created that by seeing what you wanted to see and projecting. You put him on a pedestal and became a professional red flag ignorer as a result. It's difficult to let go of the unanswered questions, the disappointment, and the could of, would of, should of, but emotional hoarding will get you nowhere.

You basically just had an orgy with your own projections. If your self-esteem was intact, you wouldn't fall in love with projections; you'd fall in love with character and distance yourself from an absence of it.

> **Character = PATTERNS (that are comprised of actions) and words that consistently MATCH those patterns in REALITY (not in your hopes, dreams, imagination, orgasms, and potential).**

We live in a time where we are more connected to our phones than ever before. Breakups are harder to go through than they have ever been in history. You can be broken up but still be able to go on your phone, check on your ex at any time, and see photos of him on social media. I know it's hard to cut that habit, and I actually have no problem with you not being able to stop the cyber snooping right at this moment. I have a problem with you viewing your ex in any way (whether it be in your mind, on his social media profile, photos that you have together, whatever it may be) through the lens of anything other than reality.

> **Your emotional gag reflex can always be found in reality, and your ex knows this. This is why he's always had to try and distort your reality.**

You can't get so "disgusted" by a good guy you go on a date with who chews his food with his mouth open or has bad breath but *then* pine over an ex whose emotional breath is so bad, it made you believe that you were unattractive, defective, and unlovable. Contradiction is the root of misery. And until you clean up this contradiction, you will continue to overvalue everything that prevents your emotional gag reflex from kicking in.

You are heartbroken but not defective. You are down but not defeated. There is a big difference. Never confuse someone's lack of respect, awareness, and emotional intelligence with what you are actually worth. Stop trying to "punish" your ex and "educate" him on what's right and what's wrong. You are not a toxicity parole officer.

> **His punishment is not about how much you can trigger his fragile ego with a hot selfie, yank his chain, and reduce your breakup to a pathetic game. His punishment is *the way he feels about himself*—every moment of every day.**

If your ex felt better about himself, he wouldn't even have *the capacity* to behave the way he has and does. He also wouldn't be so reliant on external validation or have to make up for the fragility of his ego with the hardness of his heart.

The next time you miss your ex and think he looks so much happier and more attractive in a newly posted photo, please don't go on some reactive tirade. Don't let it ruin your day and your reputation.

You just need to stay on your White Horse and calmly remind yourself of what you *already know* his capacities are.

Stay in that space of honesty and allow disgust to sink in.

It can be scary, but it will set you free.

12

Getting Revenge and Making Sure He Regrets Losing You

Posting indirect photos or quotes on social media to take a petty stab at your ex can be fun. But do you know what's even more fun than sticking up a digital middle finger?

> **Dropping a bomb that kills all the grass he was so convinced was greener.**

That bomb is made up of your success, your indifference, and your ability to be everything that your ex has consistently proven he isn't—genuinely happy, emotionally intelligent, honest, unbothered, and consistent. Someone who loves their younger self unconditionally and will go to the ends of the earth to choose and protect that child. Someone whose boundaries preserve her peace and mental health. Someone who knows that her triggers are not her truth and, because of this, is no longer a slave to her ego.

Instead of being bitter and insecure, be grateful for the education he gave you in everything you don't want and will no longer tolerate.

Winning this breakup starts and ends with making the decision to STOP.

STOP sending paragraph-long text messages; STOP sending any text messages at all! STOP asking questions that you *already* know the answers to. STOP begging for closure and fishing for reactions. STOP beating yourself up. STOP feeling guilty for finally hitting your limit. You did the best you could. And you can't beg your way into being "The One That Got Away." Nor will you *ever* be able to apologize your way into the relationship and life you deserve. STOP worrying that your ex will change and be happier without you—he's unhappy with *himself*. STOP entertaining stupidity and enabling idiots. You are doing the right thing by making the decision to cut. him. off.

There is nothing your ex can say that would ever justify what he did. What more do you want? *You are already in possession of everything that you are looking for.*

The benefit of the doubt window has closed; the chances have run out. If your ex thinks that you are a "bad person" for finally implementing boundaries and dignifiedly ACTING on his lies, excuses, and manipulations, that's not your problem. Stay on your White Horse and keep going. His ego is counting on you to give up on *yourself*, never him. And as long as you are insecure, desperate, and crumb hungry, he can keep feeling like the winner of this breakup—who is secure in his decisions, superior to you, and egoically fed.

I understand that you want revenge. You have every right to want to see your ex pay for what he's put you through. But the only way to get the kind of revenge you are looking for is by letting *him* have the last word and cutting all forms of contact. You don't need to have "the final say" or try to leave with "the power" and keep allowing him to make you look like a fool.

There has to be more than one person to play a game, and you are DONE with the back-and-forth.

Breakups with toxic people are not won by playing games. They're won by walking away and cutting contact; by giving up on trying to resuscitate the corpse of a person that never was. They're won by accepting who your ex has proven himself to be, surrendering to what is, adjusting your boundaries accordingly, and cutting off all access that he has to you.

I am often asked if I believe in revenge, and I most certainly do. I always get even. But I'm not a proponent of getting off your White Horse in the name of revenge.

The best revenge is taking a mental inventory of everything that someone who broke you is NOT and making the decision to become all of those things. It's SHOWING (not desperately posting on social media or telling) toxic people how much of a launching pad their absence really is. It's about building a life as a result of the awareness, self-reliance, and self-love that their bullshit gave you no choice but to grow. This is the scariest, most difficult thing to do, but it will reward you in spades.

When faced with something painful, we will generally try to fight the current, flee from the scene, or freeze. Do not freeze. There is nothing but death and defeat in the frozen. The only way you can "fight" for your right to be respected and WIN this breakup is by fleeing—not in an attempt to be avoidant or get your ex to chase you; not to cause a big drama but to protect *your younger self* and get the fuck away from what is poisonous to *your* system.

Everything you want your ex to feel and realize will not happen in your presence. It can only happen in your absence.

And even then, the "missing" you and the "realizations" on your ex's part will only be a by-product of selfish regret and panic because he feels so *out of control*. It's no different than a toddler throwing a tantrum because the old toy they discarded for a shiny new one is looking a lot better (and proving to be an irreplaceable CLASSIC) now that the new one isn't so new anymore. So the toddler wants to get the toy back.

Well, I'm sorry to say, life doesn't work like that in the adult world.

Do not beat yourself up over how much you gave, what you put up with, and how nice you were despite being treated terribly. You also don't need to obsess over the times you reacted in ways that made you look crazy and feel weak.

When you cut contact with a toxic person, their curiosity starts to fog up the memories that would otherwise keep their ego fed. **And they can only feed off those memories for so long.** In this way, everything you've been beating yourself up for will end up working that much more in your favor because it makes your absence (and the silence associated with it) that much louder.

I hear from a lot of people that it's best to "wish your ex well," "send him peace," and "hope that he finds happiness." This approach does not work for me. There are many people I've treated poorly and many who have treated me poorly in my life. When I think of the people who hurt me, I don't wish them well or ill.

I simply feel *nothing*. And I wish the same kind of indifference and peace for those whom I have hurt.

I've coached thousands of people who struggle with shame over feeling very human emotions of "I'll show them" after being in a toxic relationship. And if spiteful feelings are your initial fuel to dignifiedly get to a place where you can now, truly choose yourself (and ultimately reach indifference); *what's so wrong with that?*

It's not always easy to just choose yourself and "wish them well" after a breakup. It's also not helpful to pretend that the process is linear. Which leads us to...

THE NO-CONTACT RULE

The "No-Contact Rule" is something that we are all familiar with post-breakup. You use the no-contact period to grieve your relationship. And with every day that you remain in no contact, you start to view your ex in the light of *reality* as opposed to the filter of self-blame and desperation. Not every breakup requires that you go no contact, but I have found that it is necessary to implement after breaking up with a toxic person who does not respect your boundaries. Many resources online literally sell the No-Contact Rule as a way to get your ex back. I have two issues with this:

1. If it takes you having to cut your ex completely off for him to be a decent human being who is honest with you and recognizes your worth, you need to ask yourself, "Do I want to be with a man, or do I want

to have an unruly teenage son?" "Do I want to be a partner in a mutual and adult relationship, or do I want to be a managerial mommy who ends up being the taken-for-granted doormat because she loves without conditions?"

2. If you implement the No-Contact Rule with your ex just to get him to react, freak out, and want you back, you are essentially communicating through your actions that you are okay with your "soulmate" equating a loss of control over you with genuinely wanting to respect and commit to you.

Going no contact is about making the decision to walk away *in light* of having your own back *in spite* of your libido, head, and heart being in a state of triggered reactivity. Your triggers will try everything to fear-monger you into believing that your ex is the sole supplier of your emotional oxygen. He's not. Cutting contact gives you the space to create your own closure so that you can heal, deal, and become the C.E.O. of YOU. It allows you to process your feelings and ultimately build an incredible life with gratitude because you know just how bad it can be.

This isn't about a set amount of time or a certain tactic. And it should never be about eliciting a reaction or being hurtful and spiteful. You are gracefully accepting (through your *actions*) that this person cannot give you what you want and deserve.

If I make the decision to cut contact with someone, I never feel bad about it because their behavior gave me no choice. I no longer base my worth on someone handing me scissors. That's on them. What am I supposed to do with scissors? Put them in my pocket and risk further injury? Scissors are meant to *cut*, not to put in your pocket so you have a license to be a victim, feel sorry for yourself, or throw back in an attempt to cause pain. View people's hurtful and disrespectful behavior as the gift that it is and always will be: scissors to cut yourself OUT of their bullshit.

HOW LONG SHOULD YOU STAY IN NO CONTACT?

There's really no set amount of time when you cut off a toxic ex. I'm still in no contact with people from years and years ago. I don't make a concerted effort not to call them, and I'm never thinking about it. I'm just living my life. The more I love and focus on my younger self, the less I care about being an adult who has to ignore that child in order to get the validation from others that I cannot manufacture within.

You should never telephonically, technologically, or physically chase after *anyone* who has disrespected and devalued you.

Let your silence do the talking, and don't worry about him forgetting you. He won't. Think about it: when it's your birthday, whom do you remember more—everyone who wished you a happy birthday or the **one person** who didn't?

And although this could make all of the logical sense in the world, our emotions can negate logic. They can also negate reality and disable our ability to see the long-term, unfuckwithable confidence and power that is attained by staying on our White Horse and NOT pursuing short-term satisfaction. Regrettable action is always taken very quickly on emotional impulse after being triggered.

If you're contemplating getting off your White Horse, remember this: You can never be standing in the light of your own power WHILE being emotionally impulsive. It's tough enough living in a society that feeds on cracking our impulse codes and draining our wallets. Why do we keep submitting to cracking our own—all in the name of getting toxic people to validate our worth? Pointless!

If you can't cut physical contact because you work together, have a child together, or a court-ordered custody agreement, you need to cut *emotional* contact. Always be kind and professional but give the bare minimum to them. Keep the focus *entirely* on work or your child, and get out of the situation. Move on with your day. Your time is valuable.

I've gotten off my White Horse many times in the name of "sticking up for myself." It wasn't. It was my desperation at its zenith.

So how do you know what to do when you give in to your triggers and (willingly) fall right off your White Horse?

HOW do you deal when you were doing SO WELL and in a weak moment broke no contact, and now everything has gone to complete shit?

Is there any hope of ever getting your power back?

There is. And it's simple.

You are feeling pathetic, defeated, stupid, angry at yourself, and in many ways, back at square one, not knowing at all what to do. Instead of allowing these feelings to disable your emotional gag reflex from kicking in, you need to *feel* every ounce of the emotions that you're feeling.

FEEL the pain, embarrassment, and bruises. Feel the COST of getting off your White Horse.

If you don't vow to USE these feelings and this experience as propellant OUT of ever reengaging again, you'll keep engaging from the justification mentality of "What's the use? I've already ruined it" and then before you know it, find yourself in a "friends with benefits" situation.

You are not pathetic or weak. You fell off, and it's okay. One of my favorite quotes by one of my favorite people, Les Brown:

"When life knocks you down... Let your reason get you back up."

We have ALL been there. We've all lost our cool and our dignity. Allow that depletion to be your REASON to get back up and *on* your White Horse.

The ability to say "I've had enough" and back it up with consistent actions that are rooted in the respect you have for yourself is solid GOLD. The day that you're able to act on "enough" (even after taking an embarrassing tumble off your White Horse) is the day that you'll start getting your confidence and power back.

You wouldn't have picked up a book called *Win Your Breakup* if your breakup hadn't been reduced to a game that you feel like you have to win. That reduction can only occur if you were involved with someone who operates exclusively from their ego.

The only way to win a breakup with a toxic ex is to surrender and walk away.

There is a certain power in surrender and letting go. I know it sounds depressing and wrong, but stick with me here.

Right now, you need to surrender to relational defeat.

Write this on a sticky note and read it while you're looking in the mirror: "I'm sick of the stress this is putting on my mind and body. I'll take the 'L'; I don't care anymore. I may have lost a lot, but I'll be damned if I lose my mental and physical health over this."

When you don't know what to do or where to turn, think of this: The most successful C.E.O.s and the very best athletes in the world did not get to their status by *not* accepting defeat. They didn't get to the top by denying and "fact-checking" in the name of reengaging, shit-talking, or disrespecting their losses in any way. They got to that level by getting back on their White Horse, surrendering to the wounds, the unknowns, the failures, and *using* the feelings associated with defeat to propel them into unparalleled excellence (and completely shock those who defeated them in the past).

Instead of wasting their time trying to retaliate and "get back at" those they lost to, the people who made fools out of them, they got better *as a result*. They got stronger. And their LIVES (not their empty words) began to PROVE that the people they lost to in the past were nothing more than stepping-stones to greatness.

As I said earlier in Chapter 2, your ex was your northern star. And what do northern stars do? *They point you on your way to what is meant for you.* By accepting your ex as the northern star that he is, you end up becoming his karma.

I know it's hard, but you *know* what you have to do here. Please stop the insanity. Please stop the attention-mongering, the stalking, and the madness. For once, you need to prioritize your younger self over the bullshit and noise.

Day by day, the light will start to come in. You'll still hurt for most of the day, but in between that pain, you'll find your pulse again. You'll find yourself, and eventually, you'll be living a life that you didn't think was in the cards for you.

Please know that no matter how much you believe right now that you have irreparably messed up, you haven't. Time and dedication to closing your door (and bolting it shut) does wonders. You don't need to explain yourself. Make the decision to STOP and revel in the peace of that decision. The sky won't fall. And you will most likely hear from your ex again. The ego boost for him that you are falling off your White Horse is often too addicting for him not to throw crumbs at again sometime in the future.

Don't ever react to anyone who made you question your worth. They don't have anything new to say, and you don't have any more time to waste.

Forgive yourself by accepting this relational defeat so that you can be the emotional entrepreneur that your destiny has *already* deemed you as being.

You don't owe anyone anything. The only person whom you will ever owe EVERYTHING to is yourself—you owe it to your younger self to accept this defeat. Just because you couldn't grow a rose garden out of weeds, that doesn't mean you're not deserving of roses. It means that you need to get yourself into an environment where roses can actually grow.

There is nothing more you could do or give. This breakup requires *surrender* to win, not emotional warfare.

You just WON a life without your ex's toxicity.

Your ex LOST YOU; remember that. He will never again know what it's like to have you in his life.

And now you finally know what it's like to have *yourself* back in yours.

ACKNOWLEDGMENTS

To my readers, clients, and White Horse warriors all over the world, you have given me the greatest gift of all. You have made me a writer and allowed me to realize that family isn't defined by a biological connection as much as it is a soul one.

To Michael, you are the inspiration behind the kind of person I tell everyone never to settle until they find. Thank you for loving me, forgiving me, understanding me, believing in me, and not giving up on me during the times I felt like giving up on myself. You have supported every dream, every endeavor, and you have never discouraged me—even when it would have made your life much easier to do so. I don't know what I ever did to be lucky enough to know you for the last fifteen years, let alone call you my best friend and the love of my life. I am so grateful for you, your wonderful, supportive parents, and your family. I love you with all my heart and soul.

To my daughter, you are my every reason why and our dream come true. No one knows your name yet except me and Dad. We can't wait to meet you. When the day comes that I'm no longer physically here, open this book and you will find me. You'll be reminded of my love for you and have all the answers you need.

To my Mom, there is nothing I could ever write that would even begin to express how much you mean to me, how much you've taught me, and how much you've inspired me by enriching and saving the lives that you do every day. I love you and am always, only for you.

To my Father, I love and appreciate you endlessly. Every memory we have is cherished in my heart. Thank you for your support and your love.

To Dan McCarroll, you are an angel in my life and the lives of so many. You were the first person to not only hear me out but also give me a shot. I will never forget what you've done for me and this book.

To Greg Behrendt, "honored" and "surreal" are understatements in describing how it felt when you agreed to edit this book. When you told me that I did not need a developmental editor, that you would be happy to edit the manuscript, and that I could do this on my own, it was like Michael Jordan telling someone they could shoot a basketball. Greg, you have a way of empowering writers and artists in the very moment that you are kindly redirecting them. You also have a way of de-escalating and disempowering fear and doubt that I am so thankful to have been on the receiving end of. This book would not be what it is if not for you, my friend. Your recommendations, guidance, and care that went into *every* aspect of this book will always be remembered.

To Scott Jordan Harris, you are someone who makes me not only want to be better but actually gets me to believe that I can be. I wish that everyone had you in their life. You were with me throughout every part of this process—offering your invaluable professional opinions, unconditional support, and the strongest, most beautiful heart that I am so grateful to be connected to. I love and appreciate you, Scott.

To my professor, Elizabeth Dale. You noticed me when I felt invisible, you loved me when I felt unlovable, and you believed in me when I was scared to execute. Thank you for inspiring me to color outside the lines, to stick up for myself, and never allow outside opinions and behavior to dictate my worth.

To Dr. David Ahdoot, my dear Natalie, and your entire family. Because of you I never felt alone in such a big city. Thank you for opening your hearts and home to me.

To Bob, Patti, Devin, Elyse, and Paige Antin, you have all collectively and individually been there for me in ways that I thought only a biological connection could initiate. I deeply appreciate and love you all.

To Michael Sheresky at UTA, Jessica Preciado, and Connie Mableson, your kindness, patience, advice, and support have helped more than you'll ever know.

To my girls Irena, Lorelle, and Linda, your incredible guest posts kept my blog going while I worked on this book. Thank you for helping me help so many more people around the world *through* your courage to share, connect, and help others feel less alone. You are extraordinary women, and the compassion you have for yourselves has jump-started my own when I've needed it most.

To my second Dad, John. Thank you for being there for me, for loving me as much as you do your wonderful boys, and for always proving to me that laughter really is the best medicine.

To Steve, thank you for being such an incredible, trusting, and solid support from day one.

To my dearest friend, my soul sister, Tonya. There isn't anything we haven't been through, and there isn't anything I wouldn't do for you. Thank you for always inspiring me to keep going, keep building, keep trying to be a better person every day, keep learning from mistakes, and keep giving what I wish I had.

To the best friends/family a girl could ever dream of: Bridget G, Lizzie R, Janet H, Alexandra S, Spozhmai W, Catherine C, Nurit G, Cindy and Nicole A, Kato K, Blair L, Brittany A, Kelly M, Brandon P, Amanda C, Amy F, Molly H, Caitlin V, Amanda and Jill H, Juan Pablo M, Gretchen R, Alli W, Vincent A, Anna R, Jared MB, Kane H, Johnny B, Kelsey W, Lauren G, Tanya R, Jarrad H, Lori C, Dana G, Vinny M, Erin H, Carolyn C, Mik D, Renee B, Rosa L, Connie B, Greg M, Kurtis L, Riley O, Brian Y, Evan S, Gabrielle D, Moe, John and Chrissy S, Tammy G, Ted D, Bryan F, Wyatt P, Debbie B, Anna S, Garret N, Iris K, Bob B, Dorothy and Don A, and Kat J. We have been there for each other through it all—death, diagnosis, failure, success, heartbreak—and it will always be that way. I hope that I make you all feel as loved, valued, special, capable, strong, and resilient as you make me feel every day.

I would also like to thank my incredible team at Scribe, who worked tirelessly to put this book together and combine their expertise with my vision. To my author strategist (and one of my close friends), Rikki Jump, I'll always remember the day I first called you two years ago. If it weren't for your patience and empathy, I would not have made the decision to stop trying to get this book traditionally published, take on all the risk, and self-publish it. I would not own every part of this book. To my publishing manager, Kacy Wren, you are one of the most thoughtful people I've ever had the pleasure of knowing. Thank you for always going above and beyond for this baby of mine.

To my art director, Rachel Brandenburg, cover designer, Anna Dorfman, and layout designer, Ian Claudius, thank you for the most incredible design. Thank you for bringing this book to life!

To Miles Rote and Zach Obront, thank you for creating a marketing plan to get this book in the hands of even more people who need it and feel alone in their pain.

Thank you all for reading, responding, watching, listening, and connecting. Most of all, thank you for surviving. Thank you for not giving up on yourself and by doing so, allowing me to experience the gift of your presence.

Isn't it nice to know that no matter what happens, we have each other? I am eternally grateful.

Made in United States
Orlando, FL
25 April 2023

32471980R00140